Listening C1

Six more practice tests for the **Cambridge C1 Advanced**

Fiona Aish and Jo Tomlinson

PROSPERITY EDUCATION
www.prosperityeducation.net

Registered offices: Sherlock Close, Cambridge
CB3 0HP, United Kingdom

© Prosperity Education Ltd. 2024

First published 2024

ISBN: 978-1-915654-23-6

This publication is in copyright. Subject to statutory exception
and to the provisions of relevant collective licensing agreements,
no reproduction of any part may take place without the written
permission of Prosperity Education.

'Cambridge C1 Advanced' and 'CAE' are brands belonging to The Chancellor,
Masters and Scholars of the University of Cambridge and are not
associated with Prosperity Education or its products.

Designed by ORP Cambridge

Audio production by FFG Media: www.ffgmedia.co.uk
Actors: Rob and Natalie Holman, Jessica Bennett, Sandy Murray,
and Jake and Rhiana Drake.

The moral rights of the authors have been asserted in accordance with
the Copyright, Designs and Patents Act 1988.

For further information and resources, visit: www.prosperityeducation.net

To infinity and beyond.

To download the audio content:
Go to www.prosperityeducation.net/downloads
Enter password: TIAB
Select the book image
Select content to download

Contents

Introduction	4
About the C1 Advanced Listening exam	5
Test 1	7
Test 2	17
Test 3	27
Test 4	37
Test 5	47
Test 6	57
Answer keys	67
Transcript – Test 1	76
Transcript – Test 2	81
Transcript – Test 3	86
Transcript – Test 4	91
Transcript – Test 5	96
Transcript – Test 6	101

Introduction

Welcome to this edition of sample tests for the Cambridge C1 Advanced Listening, which has been written to replicate the Cambridge exam experience and has undergone rigorous expert and peer review. It comprises six C1 Advanced Listening tests, 180 individual assessments with answer keys and audio transcripts, providing a large bank of high-quality, test-practice material for candidates.

The accompanying audio files to this resource are available to download from the Prosperity Education website:

- Go to www.prosperityeducation.net/downloads
- Enter password: TIAB
- Select the book image
- Select content to download

You or your students, if you are a teacher, will hopefully enjoy the wide range of recordings and benefit from the repetitive practice, something that is key to preparing for this part of the C1 Advanced (CAE) examination.

We hope that you will find this resource a useful study aid, and we wish you all the best in preparing for the exam.

Fiona Aish and **Jo Tomlinson**

Fiona Aish and **Jo Tomlinson** are directors of Target English, a consultancy that provides tailor-made solutions in content creation, course provision, training and testing. They have co-written several leading titles in English exam preparation, and create materials and assessment resources for a range of educational providers. They are DELTA-qualified and hold MAs in ELT and Applied Linguistics and Language Testing, respectively.

About the C1 Advanced Listening

The Cambridge English C1 Advanced (CAE) examination is a timed assessment, with approximately 40 minutes assigned to the Listening section, which is worth 20% of the available grade and comprises 30 individual assessments.

The Listening section of the examination tests candidates' abilities to follow a diverse range of spoken English, and to understand the speakers' personal opinions and attitudes, specific information being conveyed and also general meaning of lengthier monologues. It is broken down in to four parts with one mark awarded to each correct answer:

- Part 1 contains three recordings of people speaking in different situations. Each recording is followed by two multiple-choice questions.

- Part 2 is a longer recording of an individual speaking about a specific topic. In each of the eight sentences that follow, a word or short phrase has been removed.

- Part 3 is a longer recording of people speaking about a specific topic. There follows six multiple-choice questions.

- Part 4 contains five short recordings of individuals speaking about a common subject. Each recording is followed by two questions tasks.

In the exam, candidates will hear each recording twice and will be given time to read the questions before the recording is played. In this resource, the recordings play only once.

For more information, visit the Cambridge Assessment English website.

Prosperity Education Ltd.
Cambridge, CB3 0HP
United Kingdom

Dear Customer,

Thank you for buying from us.

As an independent publisher, we would really appreciate it if you would leave us your honest feedback.

 Happy with your purchase? Simply log in to your Amazon account to leave a review.

 Not happy? Please reach out to our support team: admin@prosperityeducation.net

If you like our resources and what we do, please help us get our story out there.

 You can follow Prosperity Education (and in fact any of your favourite authors) on **Amazon**.

 Our **website** contains lots of free exam-practice materials and sample downloads.

 Our **Facebook** page regularly posts English language quizzes, discount codes and free stuff.

 Follow our **Instagram** stories for updates on our English teaching and learning resources.

 Subscribe to our **Youtube** channel for Listening, Speaking and Writing practice and tutorials.

I wish you all the very best for your studies.

Tom O'Reilly, Founder of Prosperity Education

PS. This resource is also available as **a PDF download** from www.prosperityeducation.net Enter the code 10PERCENTPDF at checkout for 10% off.

Cambridge C1 Advanced Listening

Test 1

Part 1   Test 1

Cambridge C1 Advanced Listening

Audio track: C1_Listening_2_1_1.mp3

You will hear three different extracts. For questions 1–6, select the best answer A, B or C. There are two questions for each extract. Read the questions carefully before playing the audio. In the exam, you will have the opportunity to listen to each recording twice.

Extract One

1   You hear two friends talking about a sporting event. What aspect of the event do they agree on?

   A   The standard of play was poor.

   B   The facilities need investment.

   C   The tickets should be more affordable.

2   The woman suggests that they should

   A   generate some negative publicity for the club.

   B   give some direct feedback to the management.

   C   enquire about the likelihood of a refund.

Extract Two

3   You hear two friends talking about learning how to make bread. How does the woman feel about it?

   A   She's pleased with her progress.

   B   She's frustrated because it's hard.

   C   She's keen on trying different recipes.

Cambridge C1 Advanced Listening

4 The man says that the key to making good bread is

   A following the instructions.

   B attending a training course.

   C taking a relaxed approach.

Extract Three

5 You hear part of a discussion between two colleagues in a travel agency. What is driving consumers' interest in eco-tourism?

   A More sustainable travel options.

   B A desire to personalise travel.

   C The role of social media in society.

6 What is the woman's view of a current trend in the tourism industry?

   A It will be replaced shortly.

   B It is attracting more attention.

   C It could have been predicted.

Cambridge C1 Advanced Listening

Part 2
Test 1
Audio track: C1_Listening_2_1_2.mp3

You will hear a man called Chris talking about a place called Bournville. For questions 7–14, complete the sentence with a word or short phrase (a maximum of three words). Read the questions carefully before playing the audio. In the exam, you will have the opportunity to listen to each recording twice.

Bournville Village

Chris thinks the Bournville village succeeded in becoming a 7)_____.

The Cadbury brothers' search for 8)_____ led to the creation of Bournville.

The houses Cadbury built were made available to employees and 9)_____.

As well as receiving good working conditions, workers also had their 10)_____ needs met.

Today, there is a 11)_____ for rental housing in Bournville village.

Because of its protected status, residents can't alter the 12)_____ of their properties without approval.

Lightmoor Village is a 13)_____ on the Bournville model.

In its planning phase, there was 14)_____ to the new village.

Cambridge C1 Advanced Listening

Part 3 　　　　　　　　　　　　　　　　　　　　　　　　　　　　Test 1
　　　　　　　　　　　　　　　　　　Audio track: C1_Listening_2_1_3.mp3

You will hear an interview in which a psychologist is talking about leadership. For questions 15–20, select the best answer A, B, C or D. Read the questions carefully before playing the audio. In the exam, you will have the opportunity to listen to each recording twice.

15　When asked for a definition of leadership, Dr. Mayer admits that

　　A　it is a term frequently misinterpreted.

　　B　it has several specific definitions.

　　C　it means different things to everyone.

　　D　it is difficult for experts to agree.

16　According to professionals, how do leaders differ from managers?

　　A　They are better able to develop trust in others.

　　B　They have outstanding communication skills.

　　C　They know what inspires people around them.

　　D　They prioritise the general over the specific.

17　Why does Dr. Mayer talk about historical figures?

　　A　To explain how leadership has developed.

　　B　To show how leadership can be misinterpreted.

　　C　To give examples of leadership from the past.

　　D　To compare and contrast leadership styles.

18　What does the presenter agree with Dr. Mayer about?

　　A　Actions create leaders, not personalities.

　　B　Some people are natural-born leaders.

　　C　Leaders share the same characteristics.

　　D　Confidence and leadership are connected.

19 What does Dr Mayer say about how childhood experiences affect leadership?

    A Unpleasant experiences are useful.

    B Variety is the biggest influence.

    C Good role models are unnecessary.

    D Positive circumstances have little impact.

20 Dr. Mayer suggests that leadership training

    A can help people fulfil their goals.

    B gives opportunities to try out new skills.

    C should be done outside the workplace.

    D may not be as useful as people think.

Cambridge C1 Advanced Listening

Part 4 Test 1
Audio track: C1_Listening_2_1_4.mp3

You will hear five short extracts in which people are talking about learning a language. Read the questions carefully before playing the audio. In the exam, you will have the opportunity to listen to each recording twice.

Task One

For questions 21–25, select from the list (A–H) their motivation to learn another language.

Task Two

For questions 26–30, select from the list (A–H) what each speaker thinks is difficult about language learning.

While you listen, you must complete both tasks.

Task One

For questions 21–25, select from the list (A–H) their motivation to learn another language.

A   To get work in a different country.

B   To give assistance to a group.

C   To get a better position at work.

D   To boost their confidence.

E   To keep mentally sharp.

F   To understand their background.

G   To communicate with new friends.

H   To make deeper connections.

Speaker 1   [21]

Speaker 2   [22]

Speaker 3   [23]

Speaker 4   [24]

Speaker 5   [25]

Task Two

For questions 26–30, select from the list (A–H) what each speaker thinks is difficult about language learning.

A   Encountering new grammar structures.

B   Speaking fluently.

C   Understanding different accents.

D   Remembering new words.

E   Finding time to study.

F   Working with a new writing system.

G   Pronouncing different words.

H   Dealing with misunderstanding.

Speaker 1   [26]

Speaker 2   [27]

Speaker 3   [28]

Speaker 4   [29]

Speaker 5   [30]

Cambridge C1 Advanced Listening

Test 2

Cambridge C1 Advanced Listening

Part 1
Test 2
Audio track: C1_Listening_2_2_1.mp3

You will hear three different extracts. For questions 1–6, select the best answer A, B or C. There are two questions for each extract. Read the questions carefully before playing the audio. In the exam, you will have the opportunity to listen to each recording twice.

Extract One

1 You hear two friends discussing ways to save money. The man implies that he

   A has had some unforeseen setbacks.
   B is struggling to make progress.
   C enjoys certain home comforts.

2 How does the woman respond to the man's suggestion?

   A She is hostile towards it.
   B She is reluctant to try it.
   C She is overwhelmed by it.

Extract Two

3 You hear part of a radio discussion between two entrepreneurs. In Jacob's view, what is the best character trait for running a business?

   A Discipline.
   B Creativity.
   C Self-awareness.

Cambridge C1 Advanced Listening

4   What does Sonia suggest for increasing the likelihood of success in business?

   A   Identifying talented employees.
   B   Concentrating on product development.
   C   Getting professional help.

Extract Three

5   You hear two friends talking about exercise. What do they conclude about the advice they've read?

   A   It's inconsistent.
   B   It's vague.
   C   It's overwhelming.

6   The man suggests that reading academic research about exercise

   A   challenges outdated beliefs.
   B   wastes valuable exercise time.
   C   enhances people's understanding.

Cambridge C1 Advanced Listening

Part 2

Test 2

Audio track: C1_Listening_2_2_2.mp3

You will hear a volunteer called Emily talking about her trip to Sri Lanka. For questions 7–14, complete the sentence with a word or short phrase (a maximum of three words). Read the questions carefully before playing the audio. In the exam, you will have the opportunity to listen to each recording twice.

Volunteering in Sri Lanka

It was a **7)**_____ that convinced Emily to volunteer in Sri Lanka.

Emily didn't manage to see a **8)**_____ during her conservation trip.

Turtles don't use their **9)**_____ for protection like other animals.

Baby turtles tend to hatch when there are **10)**_____.

Where Emily worked, **11)**_____ was the chosen method to protect turtle eggs.

Emily particularly enjoyed seeing the **12)**_____ of the turtles.

She learnt a new skill making **13)**_____ within the camp.

The most rewarding part of volunteering is the **14)**_____ of the people around you.

Cambridge C1 Advanced Listening

Part 3	Test 2
Audio track: C1_Listening_2_2_3.mp3

You will hear an interview with a doctor specialising in art therapy. For questions 15–20, select the best answer A, B, C or D. Read the questions carefully before playing the audio. In the exam, you will have the opportunity to listen to each recording twice.

15   Dr. Chambers asserts that art therapy can be surprisingly effective in

   A   reducing recovery time.
   B   coping with severe pain.
   C   improving mental health.
   D   increasing physical strength.

16   What do studies say about implementing art therapy in healthcare?

   A   It complements other approaches.
   B   It is better than other relaxing activities.
   C   It helps medical staff understand pain levels.
   D   It improves patients' recovery time.

17   Art therapy is more effective than meditation because it

   A   generates more positive reactions.
   B   helps communicate complex feelings.
   C   produces objects that are permanent.
   D   increases patients' pain awareness.

18   How does she feel about the future of art therapy in addressing crime rates?

   A   Cautious of making predictions.
   B   Frustrated that it may be abandoned.
   C   Worried that it's too controversial.
   D   Convinced that it will remain in use.

19 People who use art therapy with children acknowledge that

   A it requires prolonged effort to work.

   B evidence for it is not overwhelming.

   C its usage is not prominent enough.

   D knowing when to use it is a delicate matter.

20 What does Dr. Chambers imply overall about art as a form of therapy?

   A Only experienced professionals should use it.

   B Its implementation should be strictly controlled.

   C Society ought to take it more seriously.

   D It has a promising future in clinical situations.

Cambridge C1 Advanced Listening

Part 4 					Test 2
Audio track: C1_Listening_2_2_4.mp3

You will hear five short extracts in which people are talking about commuting. Read the questions carefully before playing the audio. In the exam, you will have the opportunity to listen to each recording twice.

Task One

For questions 21–25, select from the list (A–H) how each speaker feels about commuting.

Task Two

For questions 26–30, select from the list (A–H) what annoys them about commuting.

While you listen, you must complete both tasks.

Task One

For questions 21–25, select from the list (A–H) how each speaker feels about commuting.

A Finds it addictive

B Doesn't miss it

C Thinks it's wasted time

D Enjoys the break

E Helps fitness

F Makes them miserable

G Finds it stressful

H Makes the most of it

Speaker 1 [21]
Speaker 2 [22]
Speaker 3 [23]
Speaker 4 [24]
Speaker 5 [25]

Task Two

For questions 26–30, select from the list (A–H) what annoys them about commuting.

A Other commuters

B Traffic

C Unreliable transport

D Motorists

E Overcrowding

F Cost

G Weather

H Cyclists

Speaker 1 [26]
Speaker 2 [27]
Speaker 3 [28]
Speaker 4 [29]
Speaker 5 [30]

Cambridge C1 Advanced Listening

Test 3

Part 1
Cambridge C1 Advanced Listening
Test 3
Audio track: C1_Listening_2_3_1.mp3

You will hear three different extracts. For questions 1–6, select the best answer A, B or C. There are two questions for each extract. Read the questions carefully before playing the audio. In the exam, you will have the opportunity to listen to each recording twice.

Extract One

1   You hear a student talking to his tutor about a project. He is having trouble

     A communicating his design clearly.

     B understanding the marking system.

     C determining the correct focus.

2   What insight does Dr. Wilson provide into what makes a good project?

     A Criticising a range of theories

     B Maintaining perspective

     C Providing extensive analysis

Extract Two

3   What does the man hope to achieve from joining the walking club?

     A Improved stamina

     B A sharper mind

     C A toned body

Cambridge C1 Advanced Listening

4 You hear two friends talking about walking as exercise. What aspect of walking do they have different views on?

   A   Why walking is beneficial.
   B   How best to sustain the habit.
   C   The impact on mental health.

Extract Three

5 You hear part of a radio programme about magazines. According to the woman, specialist magazines became widespread due to

   A   changes in employment.
   B   increased personal wealth.
   C   new publishing technology.

6 What does the woman say about specialist magazines?

   A   New titles are appearing all the time.
   B   Traditional topics are the most profitable.
   C   Consumer tastes follow social change.

Part 2
Test 2
Audio track: C1_Listening_2_3_2.mp3

You will hear a dog trainer called Kyle talking about his job. For questions 7–14, complete the sentence with a word or short phrase (a maximum of three words). Read the questions carefully before playing the audio. In the exam, you will have the opportunity to listen to each recording twice.

Being a dog trainer

Kyle thinks **7)**_____ is the most important quality of a good dog trainer.

In his first job, he noted that dogs had diverse responses upon seeing **8)**_____.

Kyle got his strict training methods from **9)**_____ initially.

Research into wolves incorrectly assumed that they tend to seek out **10)**_____.

Kyle changed his approach to focus on the **11)**_____ of bad behaviour.

Last year Kyle worked with a dog who wanted **12)**_____ from people around it.

In the first stages of training, Kyle's role is to **13)**_____.

The **14)**_____ involved in training dogs makes the job especially interesting.

Cambridge C1 Advanced Listening

Part 3
Test 3
Audio track: C1_Listening_2_3_3.mp3

You will hear an interview in which two technology experts are talking about Google Maps. For questions 15–20, select the best answer A, B, C or D. Read the questions carefully before playing the audio. In the exam, you will have the opportunity to listen to each recording twice.

15   David believes that recent developments to Google Maps have been

   A   somewhat useful.

   B   entirely predictable.

   C   utterly remarkable.

   D   immensely popular

16   What aspect of technology does David want to highlight?

   A   People are unaware of how it works.

   B   People constantly find new applications for it.

   C   People use it primarily to make their lives easier.

   D   People have become too dependent on it.

17   In Rosa's opinion, one of the greatest impacts of Google Maps is that it

   A   is a tool that is always evolving.

   B   can show where natural disasters occur.

   C   is reducing costs for rescue teams.

   D   has contributed to saving many lives.

18   How does Rosa feel about how an indigenous community used Google Maps?

   A   She is irritated that it was necessary.

   B   She is impressed by their idea.

   C   She objects to using it this way.

   D   She was disappointed with the result.

19 According to David, how might environmental data collection change society?

- **A** Companies may increase profits.
- **B** Laws could be updated.
- **C** Citizens might be healthier.
- **D** Green energy could improve.

20 Both David and Rosa are firm believers that technology

- **A** has yet to reach its potential.
- **B** can be used for the common good.
- **C** should be exploited whenever possible.
- **D** will solve environmental issues.

Cambridge C1 Advanced Listening

Part 4   Test 3
                                                    Audio track: C1_Listening_2_3_4.mp3

You will hear five short extracts in which people are talking about working in the music business. Read the questions carefully before playing the audio. In the exam, you will have the opportunity to listen to each recording twice.

Task One

For questions 21–25, select from the list (A–H) how each speaker got started in the music business.

Task Two

For questions 26–30, select from the list (A–H) the most difficult part of their job.

While you listen, you must complete both tasks.

Task One

For questions 21–25, select from the list (A–H) how each speaker got started in the music business.

A From a chance encounter

B After a training course

C From an acting audition

D Helping another musician

E Working in a studio

F At a social event

G Sending in samples

H In a talent show

Speaker 1 [21]
Speaker 2 [22]
Speaker 3 [23]
Speaker 4 [24]
Speaker 5 [25]

Task Two

For questions 26–30, select from the list (A–H) the most difficult part of their job.

A Busy schedules

B Some musicians

C Being famous

D Lack of control

E Managing income

F Travelling a lot

G Staying positive

H Continued success

Speaker 1 [26]
Speaker 2 [27]
Speaker 3 [28]
Speaker 4 [29]
Speaker 5 [30]

Cambridge C1 Advanced Listening

Test 4

Cambridge C1 Advanced Listening

Part 1   Test 4
                                     Audio track: C1_Listening_2_4_1.mp3

You will hear three different extracts. For questions 1–6, select the best answer A, B or C. There are two questions for each extract. Read the questions carefully before playing the audio. In the exam, you will have the opportunity to listen to each recording twice.

Extract One

1   You overhear a woman talking about her new house with a friend. They both agree that

   A   modern houses lack individuality.
   B   detached houses are desirable.
   C   apartment buildings are unattractive.

2   What does the man suggest with regard to the proposed house renovations?

   A   They're not in keeping with the style.
   B   They need to be done urgently.
   C   They should retain the old features.

Extract Two

3   You hear part of a conversation between a hotel employee and a guest. What is the man's assessment of the hotel so far?

   A   It has exceeded his expectations.
   B   It is unlike anywhere else he's been.
   C   It isn't easy to put into words.

Cambridge C1 Advanced Listening

4   What intriguing aspect of the hotel's history does the woman highlight?

   A   The fact that the building is still standing.
   B   How the surrounding land became a national park.
   C   The international reputation it has gained.

Extract Three

5   You hear a radio interview with a scientist about sleep. What does the woman say about people who claim to need little sleep?

   A   They believe they're extraordinary.
   B   They are distorting information.
   C   They have overestimated the time.

6   From what the woman says about sleep research, what can be concluded?

   A   Recent findings have been misunderstood.
   B   Scientists know very little about sleep.
   C   Sleep experiments are unreliable.

Part 2   Test 4
                               Audio track: C1_Listening_2_4_2.mp3

You will hear a researcher called Chloe talking about first impressions. For questions 7–14, complete the sentence with a word or short phrase (a maximum of three words). Read the questions carefully before playing the audio. In the exam, you will have the opportunity to listen to each recording twice.

First impressions

Making a good first impression is down to using our 7)_____.

Our eyes transmit our 8)_____ to the person we are speaking with.

Eye contact also is shown to improve our 9)_____.

A 10)_____ can easily be spotted when you meet someone new.

Before meeting new people, think of some 11)_____ you can use.

The speaker suggests avoiding any questions that are related to 12)_____

Show you are listening by responding appropriately and giving 13)_____.

You can also turn your 14)_____ into an asset simply by sharing them.

Cambridge C1 Advanced Listening

Part 3   Test 4
                                                          Audio track: C1_Listening_2_4_3.mp3

You will hear an interview in which two conservationists are talking about birds. For questions 15–20, select the best answer A, B, C or D. Read the questions carefully before playing the audio. In the exam, you will have the opportunity to listen to each recording twice.

15   How do the conservationists feel about the future of birds?

     A   The outlook is positive.
     B   There is a long way to go.
     C   It is too early to tell.
     D   Any progress will be slow.

16   Why does Philippa talk about the situation with one specific bird?

     A   To emphasise that conservation is hard.
     B   To raise awareness of a problem.
     C   To explain the role of zoos.
     D   To highlight what can be achieved.

17   What aspect of conservation does Matteo and Philippa disagree about?

     A   Where to focus scarce resources
     B   Why some birds need more protection.
     C   How to engage the general public.
     D   Which parts of the world are more at risk.

18   What is Philippa's opinion about the role of large species in bird conservation?

     A   They have cultural significance.
     B   They increase financial donations.
     C   They help raise public awareness.
     D   They encourage people to volunteer.

19 Matteo points out that small scale efforts in conservation

  A require a lot of volunteers.
  B need more investment.
  C can be underestimated.
  D have caused noticeable changes.

20 The conservationists advise businesses and individuals to bear in mind that

  A it is important to seek expert advice.
  B solutions do not need to be complex.
  C many cities provide assistance for residents.
  D local governments should be actively involved.

Cambridge C1 Advanced Listening

Part 4   Test 4
                                                                        Audio track: C1_Listening_2_4_4.mp3

You will hear five short extracts in which people are talking about using social media at work. Read the questions carefully before playing the audio. In the exam, you will have the opportunity to listen to each recording twice.

Task One

For questions 21–25, select from the list (A–H) the role social media has in their job.

Task Two

For questions 26–30, select from the list (A–H) what advice each speaker gives about using social media.

While you listen, you must complete both tasks.

Task One

For questions 21–25, select from the list (A–H) the role social media has in their job.

A Replying to complaints

B Getting customers

C Highlighting products

D Raising their profile

E Giving advice

F Doing market research

G Managing reputation

H Building networks

Speaker 1 [21]
Speaker 2 [22]
Speaker 3 [23]
Speaker 4 [24]
Speaker 5 [25]

Task Two

For questions 26–30, select from the list (A–H) what advice each speaker gives about using social media.

A Use it sparingly

B Get professional help

C Think of your audience

D Consider replies carefully

E Check everything

F Do your research

G Be friendly

H Use your imagination

Speaker 1 [26]
Speaker 2 [27]
Speaker 3 [28]
Speaker 4 [29]
Speaker 5 [30]

Cambridge C1 Advanced Listening

Test 5

Cambridge C1 Advanced Listening

Part 1
Test 5
Audio track: C1_Listening_2_5_1.mp3

You will hear three different extracts. For questions 1–6, select the best answer A, B or C. There are two questions for each extract. Read the questions carefully before playing the audio. In the exam, you will have the opportunity to listen to each recording twice.

Extract One

1   You hear two writers discussing inspiration. They both agree that inspiration

    A   often appears when least expected.

    B   doesn't come naturally to everyone.

    C   requires certain conditions to thrive.

2   The woman wants to borrow the man's idea for her training course to show that

    A   writing is not a linear process.

    B   stories must engage a wide audience.

    C   inspiration is not always productive.

Extract Two

3   You hear a man talking about applying for a promotion with a colleague. The woman believes that he

    A   would rise to the challenge.

    B   underestimates his abilities.

    C   is overqualified for the role.

Cambridge C1 Advanced Listening

4 How does the man feel about the woman's opinions?

  A thoughtful

  B reassured

  C unconvinced

Extract Three

5 You hear a conversation between two friends about social media. Which view of social media does the man criticise?

  A It is a terrible distraction.

  B It is to blame for everything.

  C It is damaging communication.

6 What point about social media do the speakers agree on?

  A Some people use it responsibly.

  B It has a range of useful functions.

  C Many claims are exaggerated.

Part 2   Test 5
Audio track: C1_Listening_2_5_2.mp3

You will hear a woman called Monica talking about her job in the film industry. For questions 7–14, complete the sentence with a word or short phrase (a maximum of three words). Read the questions carefully before playing the audio. In the exam, you will have the opportunity to listen to each recording twice.

Script-supervising

Monica's job informally involves being a **7)**_____ for the director.

She needs to note down any **8)**_____ from scene to scene.

Filming **9)**_____ is particularly difficult to organise.

The fundamental reason for her notes is to ensure the clarity of the **10)**_____.

Before she works on the film, she needs to find out the **11)**_____ of the overall production.

The speaker talks about how the **12)**_____ placement in Forrest Gump could distract viewers.

Many script supervisors work their way up from being a **13)**_____.

Working in film generally doesn't have much **14)**_____, but it can be very rewarding.

Cambridge C1 Advanced Listening

Part 3
Test 5
Audio track: C1_Listening_2_5_3.mp3

You will hear part of a radio discussion in which two food writers are talking about their interest in global tea culture. For questions 15–20, select the best answer A, B, C or D. Read the questions carefully before playing the audio. In the exam, you will have the opportunity to listen to each recording twice.

15 What motivated Oliver to become a writer focusing on tea?

    A An interest in plants and medicine.

    B An article in a vegetarian magazine.

    C A change in his personal tastes.

    D An unexpected travel experience.

16 Both writers believe that people are interested in tea nowadays due to

    A the fashion for all things from Asian cultures.

    B the availability of cheap brands.

    C a shift in its cultural status in Europe.

    D a renewed interest in its therapeutic qualities.

17 What does Oliver say about traveling as a writer?

    A He has experienced cultural differences.

    B He wishes he'd had better connections.

    C He was always welcomed wherever he went.

    D He has witnessed many traditions vanish.

18 How does Leah feel about some tea traditions around the world?

    A She worries that they will soon be replaced.

    B She doubts that they ever really existed

    C She suspects that they are exaggerated.

    D She thinks that they should be better supported.

19 Leah suggests that Oliver's example of loose tea helps to explain

    A which tea is more ethical.

    B how marketing works.

    C where consumers shop

    D why trends have changed.

20 When it comes to tea culture, Oliver concludes that writers

    A probably know it all inside out.

    B take issue with scientific findings.

    C are unsure about what the future holds.

    D feel like there's plenty to learn.

Cambridge C1 Advanced Listening

Part 4   Test 5
                              Audio track: C1_Listening_2_5_4.mp3

You will hear five short extracts in which people are talking about their gap year. Read the questions carefully before playing the audio. In the exam, you will have the opportunity to listen to each recording twice.

Task One

For questions 21–25, select from the list (A–H) what each speaker did.

Task Two

For questions 26–30, select from the list (A–H) what advice each speaker gives for people going on a gap year.

While you listen, you must complete both tasks.

Task One

For questions 21–25, select from the list (A–H) what each speaker did.

A   volunteering with children

B   learning a language

C   working with animals

D   working online

E   travelling with friends

F   teaching overseas

G   working in a hotel

H   learning survival skills

Speaker 1 [21]
Speaker 2 [22]
Speaker 3 [23]
Speaker 4 [24]
Speaker 5 [25]

Task Two

For questions 26–30, select from the list (A–H) what advice each speaker gives for people going on a gap year.

A   Try to relax

B   Plan carefully

C   Think about your hobbies

D   Save up beforehand

E   Push your limits

F   Do something constructive

G   Think about money

H   Keep an open mind

Speaker 1 [26]
Speaker 2 [27]
Speaker 3 [28]
Speaker 4 [29]
Speaker 5 [30]

Cambridge C1 Advanced Listening

Test 6

Cambridge C1 Advanced Listening

Part 1

Test 6
Audio track: C1_Listening_2_6_1.mp3

You will hear three different extracts. For questions 1–6, select the best answer A, B or C. There are two questions for each extract. Read the questions carefully before playing the audio. In the exam, you will have the opportunity to listen to each recording twice.

Extract One

1   You hear a discussion between a tour guide and a tourist. What advice does the guide give the family about the waterfall hike?

   A   To keep an eye out for it.
   B   To give it a miss.
   C   To bear the weather in mind.

2   What observation is made about the visitor centre?

   A   The tour does not enhance the experience
   B   Tourists are welcome to turn up unannounced.
   C   Young people find the exhibits engaging.

Extract Two

3   You hear a woman telling a friend about finding a childhood toy. What does she decide she wants to do with it?

   A   Sell it at an antiques market.
   B   Keep it in the family.
   C   Give it to a children's home.

Cambridge C1 Advanced Listening

4   How does the woman feel about the toy?

   A   surprised it still exists.

   B   disappointed at its value.

   C   emotionally attached to it.

Extract Three

5   You hear part of an interview with a TV presenter about her new show. The presenter acknowledges that her recent jobs

   A   bear little resemblance to each other.

   B   cross over to a certain extent.

   C   have been outside her comfort zone.

6   The presenter attributes the positive feedback she has received to her

   A   background.

   B   approach.

   C   dedication.

Cambridge C1 Advanced Listening

Part 2 Test 6
Audio track: C1_Listening_2_6_2.mp3

You will hear a researcher called Jane talking about exploring the deep sea. For questions 7–14, complete the sentence with a word or short phrase (a maximum of three words). Read the questions carefully before playing the audio. In the exam, you will have the opportunity to listen to each recording twice.

Deep-sea exploration

Jane decided he wanted to work researching the deep sea when she saw a 7)_____.

The 8)_____ of ALVIN have all been completely changed.

While the images of the *Titanic* were gathered, ALVIN waited on the 9)_____.

The 10)_____ in ALVIN is done in darkness.

The head scientist on the submersible is the 11)_____.

12)_____ change depending on their geological location.

The researchers are most busy on the 13)_____.

Because of the onboard environment, the consumption of 14)_____ is forbidden.

Cambridge C1 Advanced Listening

Part 3
Test 6
Audio track: C1_Listening_2_6_3.mp3

You will hear part of a radio discussion about cycling schemes with two experts in cycling and safety. For questions 15–20, select the best answer A, B, C or D. Read the questions carefully before playing the audio. In the exam, you will have the opportunity to listen to each recording twice.

15 What does Gina mention as a contributing factor to more people cycling in cities?

    A The influence of data about accidents.

    B A psychological effect caused by less traffic.

    C A desire to improve their environment.

    D The fact that modern bicycles are safer.

16 One group of road users changed their minds about cycle schemes because

    A it made business sense.

    B of a positive campaign.

    C they were given incorrect information.

    D their journeys became easier.

17 What point do both speakers emphasise about cycle schemes?

    A Experts are not always right.

    B Not all cities are suitable.

    C Results won't be seen overnight.

    D The need for careful planning.

18 Gina suggests that cycle schemes

    A take time to reduce accidents.

    B should be implemented more quickly.

    C are more complex than people think.

    D make drivers concentrate more.

19 What aspect of cycle schemes does Julian feel is neglected?

    A Ensuring they are kept in good condition.

    B Deciding the best location for the lanes.

    C Explaining how to ride in bad weather.

    D Promoting them to local residents.

20 According to both speakers, designers of cycle schemes should

    A base their designs on those in other cities.

    B make sure that their designs are attractive.

    C focus on meeting specific location needs.

    D ask local residents to contribute their ideas.

Cambridge C1 Advanced Listening

Part 4	Test 6

Audio track: C1_Listening_2_6_4.mp3

You will hear five short extracts in which people are talking about learning to cook. Read the questions carefully before playing the audio. In the exam, you will have the opportunity to listen to each recording twice.

Task One

For questions 21–25, select from the list (A–H) how each speaker learnt to cook.

Task Two

For questions 26–30, select from the list (A–H) an advantage each speaker gives of being able to cook.

While you listen, you must complete both tasks.

Task One

For questions 21–25, select from the list (A–H) how each speaker learnt to cook.

A Taking classes

B Being inventive

C Helping their parents

D Learning from friends

E Work-based training

F Using books

G From the internet

H Watching TV

Speaker 1 [21]

Speaker 2 [22]

Speaker 3 [23]

Speaker 4 [24]

Speaker 5 [25]

Task Two

For questions 26–30, select from the list (A–H) an advantage each speaker gives of being able to cook.

A Being independent

B Boosting confidence

C Having fun

D Understanding quality

E Saving money

F Improving organisation

G Feeling relaxed

H Understanding ingredients

Speaker 1 [26]

Speaker 2 [27]

Speaker 3 [28]

Speaker 4 [29]

Speaker 5 [30]

Cambridge C1 Advanced Listening

Answers

Cambridge C1 Advanced Listening

Test 1

Part 1							
1	B	2	A	3	A	4	C
5	B	6	C				

Part 2	
7	model community
8	(new) premises
9	the (wider) public
10	medical
11	(long) waiting list
12	external appearance
13	modern twist
14	opposition

Part 3					
15	C	16	D	17	B
18	A	19	D	20	D

Part 4					
21	E	22	H	23	A
24	D	25	B	26	C
27	G	28	H	29	E
30	D				

Answers

Test 2

Part 1							
1	C	2	B	3	C	4	C
5	A	6	B				

Part 2	
7	(nature) documentary
8	lion
9	shells
10	fewer threats
11	relocation
12	first steps
13	repairs
14	commitment

Part 3					
15	B	16	A	17	C
18	D	19	A	20	C

Part 4					
21	D	22	F	23	H
24	E	25	B	26	H
27	E	28	F	29	A
30	B				

Cambridge C1 Advanced Listening

Test 3

Part 1							
1	C	2	B	3	B	4	A
5	A	6	C				

Part 2	
7	confidence
8	vets
9	(some) colleagues
10	conflict
11	(root) causes
12	attention
13	take the lead
14	obstacles

Part 3					
15	C	16	A	17	D
18	B	19	B	20	B

Part 4					
21	B	22	E	23	G
24	A	25	C	26	B
27	G	28	A	29	D
30	H				

Answers

Test 4

Part 1							
1	B	2	A	3	A	4	A
5	C	6	B				

Part 2	
7	common sense
8	emotional states
9	memory
10	fake smile
11	interesting conversation starters
12	salary
13	non-verbal clues
14	weaknesses

Part 3					
15	A	16	D	17	A
18	C	19	C	20	B

Part 4					
21	D	22	A	23	G
24	F	25	E	26	D
27	B	28	E	29	A
30	H				

Cambridge C1 Advanced Listening

Test 5

Part 1							
1	A	2	C	3	B	4	C
5	A	6	C				

Part 2	
7	backup
8	(small) changes
9	out of sequence
10	final edit
11	vision
12	iron
13	production assistant
14	job security

Part 3					
15	D	16	D	17	A
18	C	19	B	20	A

Part 4					
21	G	22	B	23	F
24	D	25	H	26	A
27	C	28	E	29	G
30	B				

Answers

Test 6

Part 1							
1	B	2	A	3	B	4	C
5	A	6	B				

Part 2	
7	coral reef
8	(original) parts
9	deck
10	descent
11	port observer
12	Collection methods
13	(main) ship
14	citrus fruits

Part 3					
15	B	16	A	17	D
18	C	19	A	20	C

Part 4					
21	G	22	B	23	H
24	C	25	A	26	D
27	G	28	B	29	A
30	E				

Cambridge C1 Advanced Listening

Transcripts

Cambridge C1 Advanced Listening

Test 1

Part 1

Audio track: C1_Listening_2_1_1.mp3

Part 1. You will hear three different extracts. For questions 1 to 6, you must choose the best answer: A, B or C. There are two questions for each extract.

Extract 1	**You hear two friends talking about a sporting event. Now look at questions 1 and 2.**
Speaker 1	I'm not sure that was the greatest performance I've ever seen. I thought they would have been more competitive, but I suppose it was entertaining enough.
Speaker 2	Well, it's my first time seeing these two players, and they impressed me, which is more than I can say for the venue itself. If it were mine, I'd throw a significant sum at upgrading and refurbishing the place, otherwise I'd be embarrassed when players like that arrived.
Speaker 1	It does look shabby and neglected, doesn't it? I'm astounded that they can attract such well-known players given the overall conditions. Actually, I think the ticket prices are unacceptable for a venue like this. I was expecting a state-of-the-art building with big screens, brand-new toilets and so on.
Speaker 2	Do you think we should email and complain, or ask for compensation like a discount next time or something?
Speaker 1	I doubt we'd have much success with that, I think we'd be better off making our feelings known on social media since large companies only seem to respond to that these days. If they think their reputation is at risk, they might offer us something.
Speaker 2	Okay, well let's give it a go and see what happens.

Extract 2	**You hear two friends talking about learning how to make bread. Now look at questions 3 and 4.**
Speaker 1	I've been trying to improve my bread-making skills recently, so I started watching some online videos.
Speaker 2	You know, I've always wanted to bake my own, but it seems very involved and I'm a bit daunted by the whole idea. Cookbooks have so many steps – I get a bit lost.
Speaker 1	Yeah. Copying someone on a video suits me better and I recently found a whole series of videos by a pastry chef which are fabulous. She goes at a slow pace, and I've been putting some of her top tips into practice, so I feel like it's all coming together now.
Speaker 2	It sounds like you're in safe hands there.
Speaker 1	Well, obviously my first few attempts were disastrous! I didn't dare let anyone try any. I don't think I was concentrating properly to be honest.
Speaker 2	Well, I mean there's a tonne of different methods and schools of thought about which one is the best if you want to get really immersed in the subject. The truth is, though, that if you don't rush it or overthink it – most loaves you make will probably turn out edible and, if you don't fancy eating one, the birds in your garden won't complain!

Transcripts

Extract 3 — **You hear part of a discussion between two colleagues in a travel agency. Now look at questions 5 and 6.**

Speaker 1 — Let's talk about another trend we should be focusing on – eco tourism. Many people now want aspects of their travel experiences to align with their values, so we need to be actively engaging with this.

Speaker 2 — And what would that entail exactly?

Speaker 1 — Well, offering alternative modes of transport (not just air or family-run accommodation for instance) for people who want to improve the local economy. Eco tourism can incorporate all sorts of different values.

Speaker 2 — Yes, I see – and actually these days people are willing to pay more for things that cater to their requirements, rather than following the herd that is mass tourism.

Speaker 1 — You know, I was reading a blog about the modern traveller saying they want to create a set of unique experiences even when visiting popular resorts or well-known cities. It's all about creating what the writer called 'Instagram moments'.

Speaker 2 — Oh yes, that's definitely fashionable – like on city breaks when people try out the street food rather than the upmarket restaurants. I suppose it was inevitable given the amount of holiday photos that people post nowadays. If you want to be noticed, you have to do something to stand out from the crowd.

Speaker 1 — And so do travel agents, so let's get to work!

Part 2

Audio track: C1_Listening_2_1_2.mp3

Part 2. You hear a man called Chris talking about a place called Bournville. For questions 7 to 14, complete the sentences with a word or short phrase.

Hi, I'm Chris O'Neill and I'm here to talk to you about a rather special place in the UK that I have lived in since I was a boy. It's called Bournville. Now, some of you might associate Bournville with chocolate, but actually it's also a village just outside Birmingham, and a rather unusual village too. While most villages grow organically, Bournville was created specifically in an attempt to establish a model community. Many people say it achieved that goal, and I'd certainly agree. So, how did Bournville come about?

Before the late 1800s, the area where Bournville stands today was just fields and a few scattered farms. However, its fate changed when brothers George and Richard Cadbury decided to locate their factory there. The famous Cadbury chocolate factory had been in a city-centre location, but the business grew too big for such an urban area, and they had to look for new premises. They decided they needed a more spacious location, one that wasn't already developed, and the area that is now known as Bournville was perfect. It was still near the city, but also had easy canal and railway access. Both of which were essential to transport the cocoa and milk for their famous chocolate.

At this time, many factory owners built housing for their workers – but the conditions and standards were usually poor and the housing was cramped. George Cadbury had a clear idea of building something more than just functional. He wanted their workers to enjoy a happy healthy life. He built houses with far superior living spaces, and with plenty of room and individual gardens. These houses were not just for the workers of the factory, either. The wider public could move there and enjoy the same living environment.

Cambridge C1 Advanced Listening

Both brothers also cared a lot about the conditions of workers in their factory. Compared to most factories in the country, their workers had high wages and good conditions, including additional benefits like pension schemes and free medical treatment were provided for all.

To this day, the village remains a popular place to live. In fact, now the area is protected and is run by a charitable company, with a lot of input from residents. It's a simple process to buy there, but there is a long waiting list for people wishing to rent, simply because so many people want to live there. There is also a strict set of rules for residents in the community.

For instance, residents can't add walls or fences, and they can't park caravans or boats on their driveways. And while they can do what they want with the internal formation of the houses, they need permission for modifications to the external appearance. Plus, everyone must pay towards the maintenance of the communal areas in the village. And there are many of these. Ever since the village was created, it has been filled with green spaces and community buildings to make life pleasant for all residents.

In fact, one survey found it to be among the nicest places to live in the whole country. No wonder it's still going strong after all these years!

This success can be seen by the construction of a second Bournville village, called Lightmoor Village. A modern twist on the original village, it has a futuristic vision but also preserves the original standards and rules. Like Bournville, it has lots of options for affordable housing, from rental to shared ownership and full ownership. However, its development wasn't particularly smooth. The village was built on a wildlife area, causing local opposition to the plan. But this didn't add much delay to planning. The charity found a solution in consultation with communities nearby to preserve nature and still create affordable housing. Hopefully, Lightmoor will have as much success as Bournville has.

Part 3

Audio track: C1_Listening_2_1_3.mp3

Part 3. You hear an interview in which a psychologist is talking about leadership. For questions 15 to 20, choose the best answer: A, B, C or D.

Interviewer	My guest today is psychologist Dr. Tim Mayer, who is here to help us understand one of the modern world's most talked-about topics: what makes a good leader? Now, Dr. Mayer, we know that leadership is essential for people in charge of sports teams, work teams and possibly in education too. Yet pinning down exactly what it involves is very challenging…
Speaker 1	Yes, this is indeed the case. Part of the reason is that good leadership is often based on how individuals interpret it for their own contexts. I mean we can draw out a few similarities between coaching a football team and managing a team of financial analysts. But those similarities soon end because of the context.
Interviewer	Yes, that does make things tricky, doesn't it? And, in your view, why is it that people often confuse leadership with management? Although they may seem the same, apparently these concepts are really quite distinct.
Speaker 1	Psychologists, life coaches and business experts usually say that what separates them is how 'abstract' they are. So, for both roles you need to be a good listener, be decisive and be able to develop trust among others. But a manager does this with a specific group of people working on defined tasks, whereas a leader does this in general. And this can be a leader in a school, a company, a sports team or even a group of volunteers.
Interviewer	So, I suppose we could say that managers execute plans and ensure that people work effectively and meet deadlines, that kind of thing? Whereas leaders give people something to believe in and inspire them to want to achieve it?

Transcripts

Speaker 1	Exactly. But I actually don't think that's the right comparison to make. In my view, the issue is more about connecting leadership with authority and having power over others. I mean there were plenty of world leaders in the past who had great leadership skills in theory, but we don't view them in a positive light. It would be better if we moved away from this.
Interviewer	Can you expand on this?
Speaker 1	I mean that in order to capture the essence of what makes a good leader, we shouldn't be describing their character traits, we should start talking about their actions instead.
Interviewer	Hmm, I see. You know, I think that if someone is willing to help others through hard work, they can be a leader regardless of their background or education. Just look at some of today's most successful businesspeople. Many of them came from humble backgrounds and they were able to get others to believe in their ideas.
Speaker 1	Yes, leaders have to be comfortable taking risks in order to inspire others and make progress. But interestingly, studies show that a good education and upbringing don't have a lot to do with good leadership in many fields. This isn't something we get taught at school or at home.
Interviewer	That's an interesting point. Finally, Dr. Mayer, could you give our listeners some advice about how to develop their leadership skills? I mean, would you recommend going on a training course, or going for a promotion at work? What are your thoughts on this?
Speaker 1	Training courses aren't usually a great investment unless they are part of the organisation you already work for, because then they are tailored to your context. Otherwise, they are too general. Something that many businesses leaders talk about is reading books about training and then practising the skills in your current role. Based on how people respond, you're likely to see if you have leadership potential in the future.
Interviewer	Well, I'm afraid that's all we have time for today. Many thanks for coming in Dr. Tim Mayer.

Part 4

Audio track: C1_Listening_2_1_4.mp3

Part 4. You hear five short extracts in which people are talking about learning a language. For questions 21 to 30, choose from the list A–H.

Extract 1	My work life was always so busy that I couldn't devote any time towards learning another language, although I'd always wanted to. So, when I retired, I thought: why not? After all, as they say, 'use it or lose it'. I wanted to keep my brain in gear, so I started French classes as France was always a beloved holiday destination for me. Well, I'm six years into studying and I've come on leaps and bounds. I chat away to the locals now when I'm there, although I don't always pick up what they're saying back to me, depending on where they are from. That's probably one of the trickiest things about language learning – in reality most people don't speak like they do in the textbooks!
Extract 2	As a reporter on international affairs, one element of my work is to get people to open up to me. That's why, when I was stationed in China, I tried to immerse myself more in the community by learning Chinese. I didn't bargain on how difficult it would be! Of course, they have a different alphabet, but that wasn't even the most complicated part. I couldn't, and still can't, get my mouth around the sound of some of the words. I hope there is some improvement soon and I become more intelligible!

Cambridge C1 Advanced Listening

Extract 3 I married my Italian wife over eight years ago, but it wasn't until last year that we decided to relocate to Italy. That's when I knew I'd need to pick up Italian properly. After all, who would hire me if I couldn't even speak the language? I'm fortunate as I get to practise every day with my wife and her family, and I'm slowly seeing improvements. My confidence in Italian is definitely growing, but I still sometimes just nod and laugh even though I have lost the thread of the conversation. I can't seem to be able to admit that I don't always get it!

Extract 4 My parents were originally from India, and moved to the UK around 30 years ago, so I grew up listening to both English and Bengali at home. However, although I spoke Bengali, I hadn't formally learnt it, and I always felt a bit unsure of what was correct. I decided to try and squeeze in some learning and bought myself a book to brush up on the grammar. It made such a difference, and I didn't need to do a great deal as I'd learnt so much from such a young age. Nothing really stressed me about learning, except maybe trying to fit it in, but I'm really glad I made the effort.

Extract 5 I was going backpacking around South America with some university buddies, and, although one of us was half Portuguese, nobody had a word of Spanish. That's why I decided to learn the basics, and well, I just got hooked. It's such a romantic language and I saw a drastic improvement over the course of our visit. By the end, I could make myself more or less understood in a variety of situations, but I also heard so many new terms that I'm positive half of them slipped back out again straight away! I'd love to learn more, at a slower pace, now I'm back to everyday life.

Transcripts

Test 2

Part 1

Audio track: C1_Listening_2_2_1.mp3

Part 1. You will hear three different extracts. For questions 1 to 6, you must choose the best answer: A, B or C. There are two questions for each extract.

Extract 1	**You hear two friends discussing ways to save money. Now look at questions 1 and 2.**
Speaker 1	Last time we met up, you mentioned you were economising, or at least attempting to, so how's that going?
Speaker 2	Well, I've cancelled my gym membership because frankly I don't go enough to justify the fees, but, apart from that, cutting down on general expenses seems easier said than done.
Speaker 1	What about other subscriptions? I know I could do with reviewing my streaming services and food deliveries, but once you're signed up to all these wonderful lifestyle-improvement services, it's difficult to get round to cancelling them.
Speaker 2	You know, I've only got one streaming account and it doesn't cost me a great deal as I signed up during the discount period.
Speaker 1	Hmm, in that case you could try a 'no spend month'. A friend of mine did it recently and, apparently, she managed to save a fortune.
Speaker 2	But surely I have to spend *something*. What about groceries and everyday essentials like toiletries?
Speaker 1	Those are fine, but the concept is that you don't buy other random stuff just because you fancy it. Just the necessities are allowed, so no last-minute take-aways because you can't be bothered to cook, or no new clothes, etc. You get the idea.
Speaker 2	Perhaps, if all else fails, I'll give it a go.

Extract 2	**You hear part of a radio discussion between two entrepreneurs. Now look at questions 3 and 4.**
Speaker 1	Jacob, as a successful entrepreneur, what top tip would you give our listeners thinking of starting their own business?
Speaker 2	Well, Sonia, besides the obvious, don't do anything without a proper business plan – and I mean something really detailed not just a vision or an innovative product idea. I think my top tip would have to be to reflect on how you'd manage the challenges as your business develops.
Speaker 1	Like what kinds of things might be stressful or give you sleepless nights, that kind of thing?
Speaker 2	Exactly. And 'do you have strategies in place to work through the difficult times?', because there will definitely be some. Thinking about this in advance can help you work out if running a business is for you or not.
Speaker 1	Hmm. Interesting, and I completely agree.

Cambridge C1 Advanced Listening

Woman

Speaker 2   And what about you? Have you got any recommendations for our listeners?

Speaker 1   Um, I guess mine would be to work out your support requirements, especially when it comes to legal and financial stuff. Not everyone is suited to that kind of work, especially entrepreneurs who are usually more solution – or vision – focused. You'd be better off getting someone in who knows what they're doing while you get on with spending time on areas where your specific talents lie.

Extract 3   **You hear two friends talking about exercise. Now look at questions 5 and 6.**

Speaker 1   I'm having trouble trying to find time to work out. I was reading up about the best time to exercise online and it seems really complicated.

Speaker 2   I know what you mean. There's all this contradictory information from scientific studies which I found surprising. I thought it'd be relatively clear cut. I mean, some studies mention that early mornings are best, whereas others say we should exercise after lunch, so I'm at a loss really.

Speaker 1   What I noticed was that all their suggestions become clearer once you get into the details. So, apparently, morning exercise works wonders for fat burning, but there's also evidence that afternoons are the way forward for building strength. The problem is that people just give up when they can't find a definitive answer straight away.

Speaker 2   I can understand why. I mean, who wants to spend hours reading scientific studies instead of getting out and exercising? Unless of course you're a professional athlete or you're training for a specific sporting event like a match or marathon when I suspect there are benefits to be had.

                 Otherwise, why not just work out what fits into your lifestyle?

Part 2

Audio track: C1_Listening_2_2_2.mp3

Part 2. You hear a volunteer called Emily talking about her trip to Sri Lanka. For questions 7 to 14, complete the sentences with a word or short phrase.

My name's Emily Richardson, and I'm going to tell you about my recent trip to Sri Lanka, volunteering with the Wildcare organisation.

I hadn't really considered volunteering at all, even though a good friend had done it in South America and told me how amazing it was, but I changed my mind after seeing some turtles in a nature documentary. Watching how precarious their lives are at the beginning convinced me to look into volunteering, and I decided to go for it.

I wasn't disappointed. Sri Lanka is full of different kinds of wildlife and is perfect for anyone who loves animals. The island is host to leopards, sloths, crocodiles, lions and elephants. By the end of the trip, I had spotted most of these animals. I missed out on catching a glimpse of a lion, but I got to see a Sri Lankan elephant, which was a definite highlight. Unfortunately, lots of animals on the island, including the lions and elephants, are severely endangered.

The turtles I worked with are also endangered. They've inhabited the earth for millions of years, and they play a vital role in maintaining ecosystems in the sea. Male and female turtles are identical, apart from a long claw the males have, which looks quite scary. And unlike tortoises and terrapins, sea turtles can't withdraw their heads and limbs into their shells when faced with danger, although they do have quite a bite! But, like humans, some are more aggressive than others!

Despite travelling thousands of kilometres by sea, females often go back to the same stretch of beach every time they want to bury their eggs. We still don't know how they manage to navigate to the same spot. However, unlike many other types of reptiles, the female turtle doesn't stay with its eggs, but leaves them alone in the sand. The eggs remain there until they hatch. This is often at night when it's cooler and when fewer threats are present. There are plenty of dangers before getting to the hatching stage, however – for example, people sometimes take the eggs to sell on. For those eggs that make it to hatching, predators, like rats, crabs, dogs and birds are all waiting for them. Unfortunately, only one in a thousand turtles survive to adulthood, and my job was to help improve this statistic.

To protect the unhatched egg, many conservation charities use observation as a preferred method, but we didn't have the resources to do this. For us, relocation made much more sense. We would rebury the eggs in our camp and keep them safe there.

Probably the most exciting time was when the eggs were ready to hatch. I truly think there is nothing cuter than a baby turtle! Hatching was so amazing, but nothing comes close to accompanying the babies in their first steps down the beach. The joy of helping them get to the water was incredible. But my job didn't stop there: we'd also do talks about turtle conservation and show people around the camp where we worked.

It's so fulfilling knowing you are truly making a positive difference. But volunteering is so much more than that. It's also about helping out in general. I learnt to cook local Sri Lankan dishes, and also did some repairs. An ability I certainly never had before! And six months flew by in the most incredible way. For once, I wasn't glued to my phone, but spent time learning about the local culture and the varied lives of the other volunteers. All the local people treated us with kindness, but more than anything it's wonderful to see such commitment in others, where everyone puts ego and worries aside to work towards a common goal. I'd recommend it to anyone in a heartbeat!

Part 3

Audio track: C1_Listening_2_2_3.mp3

Part 3. You hear an interview with a doctor specialising in art therapy. For questions 15 to 20, choose the best answer: A, B, C or D.

Interviewer	Today I'm joined by Dr. Susan Chambers, who is going to talk to us about art therapy. Welcome, Susan.
Speaker 1	Thank you.
Interviewer	Now, some people might see art therapy as sounding a little, perhaps hippy or wishy-washy, but you're here to tell us the real facts about it, and it's far from wishy-washy…
Speaker 1	Yes, I am. Art therapy might have a bad name amongst those who know little about it, but recent research has discovered plenty of applications – not just for mental well-being, but for other, more physical ailments. More notably, I suppose, is that it's been found to be a great tool for patients with conditions that cause a lot of pain.
Interviewer	Oh, really? That *is* interesting.
Speaker 1	I mean, let's be clear, it doesn't replace the need for pain management, but it can work as a tool to help divert attention away from the pain. Some might say this is just a distraction, that perhaps you could get from listening to music or watching TV, but it's not the same. As many doctors will confirm, it's a tool to teach patients how to

Cambridge C1 Advanced Listening

	relax and manage focus, therefore altering their mood. The last thing people who suffer from chronic pain want is for the pain to control their mental state.
Interviewer	Does it work in the same way as meditation, for example?
Speaker 1	Meditation can work similarly, but it's difficult to sustain the beneficial effects afterwards. The thing about art therapy is that it helps people to be creative and take control. In a creative sense, the art can help people explore their condition as they can paint things that they relate to their pain. These pieces can then be used multiple times for therapeutic reasons, and new pieces can show how a patient is progressing on their journey.
Interviewer	Hmm, yes, I see. And are there any other arenas that we might find art therapy to be of use?
Speaker 1	Well, you might expect it to be mainly used in mental health environments, but it's also becoming an increasingly popular tool for the prison service. The prison environment is an emotional one for many offenders: they are coming to terms with their loss of freedom in an environment that may seem threatening. It's a time when they need to reconcile themselves to what they have done and what their future could be, and art is a great way to start on that journey.
Interviewer	Hmm, and what has the reaction of the general public been to this?
Speaker 1	Good, overall, and this is probably due to the fact that it's shown good results in reducing aggression, anxiety and depression in inmates. We see that those who are in the arts-therapy programmes have a much higher success rate of reintegration into society than those who do not take part in it. As with all things, a minority are against it, but this won't affect the plans to implement it further in this context.
Interviewer	And what about younger members of society? Is it useful in schools, for instance?
Speaker 1	Well, it's more restricted to being used in child psychology rather than education itself. It can really help a child open up about their problems and give psychologists great insight. Over time it can encourage younger people to express their thoughts and feelings. It helps psychologists build a relationship with them – which can sometimes be hard at first. Focussing on a fun activity like art can help to establish a connection without having to confront why the child is there.
Interviewer	Well, that's all we have time for Dr. Chambers. Thanks for talking to us today… (fade)

Part 4

Audio track: C1_Listening_2_2_4.mp3

Part 4. You hear five short extracts in which people are talking about commuting. For questions 21 to 30, choose from the list A–H.

Extract 1	My commute takes me straight through the city centre and, I have to say, some of the views are spectacular. Nobody loves commuting – it has its annoyances like anything else – but for me it's actually some much-needed time out between my job, which is quite stressful, and my four children at home. I also get to travel in the comfort of my own car, which I think helps. To be honest, there are few irritations about it, apart perhaps from the odd courier darting between the traffic and scaring the life out of me, but you can't have everything!

Transcripts

Extract 2 I know that commuting is a part of life, and millions of people do it every day, but unfortunately that doesn't make it any better for me. I quite frankly can't think of anything that lowers my spirits more than the daily chore of getting into work and back. I'm constantly crushed on the tube as everyone races to get into a space meant for half the number of people. They should really allow people to work more flexibly and take the stress off the transport system. That might at least make it a bit better.

Extract 3 Not all commutes are the same, and I think we need to think of the quality of the commute when we talk about the topic. For example, some people are in stressful, fast-paced environments catching trains while others are perhaps walking to work in the sun! For me, it's about doing something constructive, if that's possible. I always put a podcast on while I'm on the train. It helps me with the journey, but no amount of distraction can take away from the fact that the season tickets cost an arm and a leg these days. Transport companies really need to do something about that.

Extract 4 These days I work from home, but I've got to say I didn't used to think that commuting was such a chore. I used to bike to the station to catch the train and then walk to the office at the other end. Now, all I do is move from one room to the other, and although it might be easier, it certainly hasn't helped my waistline at all! I suppose one thing I don't particularly miss is how perfectly reasonable people turn into angry animals at rush hour, especially in bad weather. Everyone tries to push in front of each other, or get to the ticket barriers first. There's no need to be that keen to get to work!

Extract 5 I don't think I could tolerate a job that required me to come into an office anymore. I was over the moon to say goodbye to my daily commute, and I didn't look back. Of course, I do sometimes imagine how nice it would be to be out in the streets on a sunny day, but that's a small price to pay for having two hours of my day back. Crawling along at four miles an hour isn't exactly a laugh a minute. Of course I like driving, but certainly not that kind!

Cambridge C1 Advanced Listening

Test 3

Part 1

Audio track: C1_Listening_2_3_1.mp3

Part 1. You will hear three different extracts. For questions 1 to 6, you must choose the best answer: A, B or C. There are two questions for each extract.

Extract 1	**You hear a student talking to his tutor about a project. Now look at questions 1 and 2.**
Speaker 1	Hi Dr. Wilson. Could I clarify something about my design project as I'm having a few issues?
Speaker 2	Of course, Edward. Your project is on improving disabled access to the city park, isn't it? So, what seems to be the problem – is it the scope? Sketching out such a complex design is a difficult task.
Speaker 1	It's more that I feel I might be overly focusing on my re-design ideas instead of evaluating the park as it is now. I don't really know how much depth I should go into with the evaluation.
Speaker 2	You know, it's easy for students to get lost in their own design. After all, this is the part that is most interesting for you. However, what I want to see, as your tutor and the person who'll be grading your project, is how your analysis feeds into your design.
Speaker 1	Hmm, I see. So, what does that mean in practice?
Speaker 2	Well, step back from your work and ask yourself if you've included enough theories and background reading in this section. Your analysis of the current situation should be based on good practice in design, not just your own ideas. You need to strike a balance.
Speaker 1	That's really helpful. Thank you.
Extract 2	**You hear two friends talking about walking as exercise. Now look at questions 3 and 4.**
Speaker 1	I joined a walking club last month as I think I really need to get out and about more. I've noticed my posture is poor from all the desk work I do, so I decided to do something about it.
Speaker 2	Well, walking is said to be one of the best things for improving our overall well-being. I find that just getting out in the fresh air is all I need to reset my mind. The physical effect is positive, but for me the therapeutic results are what drive me to do it.
Speaker 1	Hmm, I hadn't thought about the mental aspects of it that much, but now you come to mention it, I do feel like some of the pressure of work has been released afterwards. Anway, my intention is to increase my overall strength so I can go on longer hikes – and reduce my cholesterol too.
Speaker 2	Those sound as though they're good goals – not too ambitious yet also easy to track and notice improvements. And if you're anything like me, this'll help to maintain your motivation.
Speaker 1	Actually, I'm someone who needs something that involves others to keep me going, rather than just plain exercise, so I think this club fits the bill perfectly.

Transcripts

Extract 3 — **You hear part of a radio programme about magazines. Now look at questions 5 and 6.**

Speaker 1 — Specialist magazines have loyal followers and stable sales even if their target audiences are small. They cover topics ranging from fishing to gadgets to jewelry-making. As an editor, Zara, could you explain how they became so popular?

Speaker 2 — Sure. They started to take off in the 1950s and 60s when technological advances started to change lifestyles across US society.

Speaker 1 — You're referring to kitchen appliances and TVs, right?

Speaker 2 — That's right, and this rush of new products into people's lives meant that new opportunities appeared for specialist magazines.

Speaker 1 — Am I right in thinking that this led to the publication of many cooking and household magazines?

Speaker 2 — Yes, but remember that people were also starting to have more leisure time as the labour market moved towards more office jobs with shorter hours. This accelerated the popularity of these magazines since people had more time to engage in their new hobbies.

Speaker 1 — Yes, I see how that would have caused an explosion in titles at the time. And I suppose that over the years as life has changed the popularity of certain magazines has shifted.

Speaker 2 — Indeed. These days, for example, you'll see lots of magazines about technology, but some topics like motoring and gardening have stood the test of time.

Part 2

Audio track: C1_Listening_2_3_2.mp3

Part 2. You hear a dog trainer called Kyle talking about his job. For questions 7 to 14, complete the sentences with a word or short phrase.

Welcome. I'm here today to talk to you about my experience as a dog trainer, so you can see if it might be a good career choice for you. Now, before I start, while a love of dogs is of course important in a job like this, the key characteristic you're going to need is confidence. And second to that, you need patience, as no dog can change overnight.

Before I became a dog trainer, I was a kennel manager. Obviously, I liked dogs, but also, I had a keen interest in why they all acted how they did. They were quite predictable around their owners, but their reaction to vets was wildly varied. Some would be petrified, others aggressive, and quite a few were actually excited and overjoyed to see them! It was far more diverse than even the way they respond to other dogs.

This got me interested in the job, but when I decided to start training, I think I went down the wrong path. I was very influenced by some colleagues who watched videos about dominant training methods. This approach was based on the belief that dogs naturally fight for a higher status, so we as trainers have to put them in their place.

These ideas, which by the way I don't follow now, were gained from watching wolf behaviour. Some researchers had claimed that wolves tend to fight over resources like food, but this study was misleading as the wolves being studied were captive, with limited resources. Wolves in the wild tend to

Cambridge C1 Advanced Listening

avoid conflict and spread themselves over larger areas if resources are limited, but absolutely let's also not forget – dogs are not wolves.

It didn't take me long to see the error of my ways. For a long time now, I've realised that, when it comes to dealing with an issue, rather than just looking at correction, it's much better to look at root causes. In fact, taking a strict approach can often make behaviour worse, or leave the dog anxious. The technique I use now is called 'positive reinforcement', and it works wonders.

I'll give you an example of a dog I worked with last year, who had a problem jumping up at anyone who came into the house. Visitors had simply stopped coming over, because, well, the dog wasn't small, and the owners really wanted to correct this. Now, people might see this dog's behaviour as dominant, demanding respect from people who came into their territory, but in reality it was the *attention* that the dog enjoyed, as he jumped up and licked them all over their faces! In this case, we can't tell the dog off, as it gives them more of what they want. We have to divert its focus.

In a case like this, we've got to get the dog to sit and stay until the visitor is inside and comfortable, and then reward the dog with snacks for being calm. At first, I play the role of the owner and the owner plays the visitor. I take the lead and model what the owner needs to do… it's about training both of them after all. The person in the visitor role has to try to ignore the dog until it's calm. Then we change, and I become the visitor so we can practise the techniques.

Of course, it's a lot of work to change a behaviour, and it doesn't happen overnight, but if the owner is willing to put the work in, you'd be surprised what a difference positive reinforcement can make. Sure, there can be obstacles, but that's what makes it such a fascinating field. If you're a problem-solver and you're interested in the psychology of animals – and their owners – this could be a perfect job for you.

Part 3

Audio track: C1_Listening_2_3_3.mp3

Part 3. You hear an interview in which two technology experts are talking about Google Maps. For questions 15 to 20, choose the best answer: A, B, C or D.

Interviewer	Today on TechTalk, we're looking at how Google Maps has changed the world, and I have experts in the field, David Franklin and Rosa Smith, to give us their insights. So, David, how did Google Maps impact our lives?
Speaker 1	Well, when it was first launched back in 2005 it meant paper maps and guidebooks weren't needed anymore. It made travel in our local neighbourhoods easier and travelling further afield less intimidating because we could get directions instantly. And this original feature has been continuously improved to the point where now we can share our location with others, even when driving. I mean, who would have thought it?
Interviewer	And, apparently, it's becoming much more than just an indispensable travel tool, is that right?
Speaker 1	Yes, it is. Although navigating our surroundings remains a key feature, others are becoming far more wide-reaching. Recommendations and suggestions for entertainment and retail are, for example, gaining ground these days. It's worth bearing in mind that we wouldn't have WhatsApp, Uber or travel apps like Expedia without the technology behind Google Maps. I wonder how many of us are conscious that along with over a million other websites, they rely on this technology to bring us their various services.
Interviewer	Well, until now I'm afraid to say I wasn't! Can I now turn to you, Rosa? As a tech journalist focusing on environmental issues, what's your take on this?
Speaker 2	Google Maps is frequently used after natural disasters to help provide critical information for rescue teams, which invariably leads to positive outcomes: things like evacuation routes or places to shelter. These data can be quickly and easily shared,

Transcripts

	saving time and helping many to reach safety. Prior to this, people working in these conditions faced a much tougher job and the likelihood of finding survivors was much less.
Interviewer	And I think you have another example of how this technology has been harnessed to combat environmental issues, Rosa?
Speaker 2	Um, yes. There are so many interesting projects to talk about: large scale, small scale and global. It's amazing the ways in which it's being used these days. But the example you're referring to is from an indigenous community in Brazil. Some years ago, they used the street view feature of Google Maps so that people could virtually paddle down the river where they live and better understand the need for environmental protection in the region. As we know, a picture can speak a thousand words, so they got a huge amount of publicity. Although it's hard to know if there was any positive impact or not.
Interviewer	Oh, that is ingenious. And David, I believe you've been writing about another interesting way Google Maps is being used.
Speaker 1	I recently became interested in how businesses and governments are using some of the latest products that have been developed from Google Maps to track other environmental issues. So, for example, air quality, pollen levels and the potential output of solar panels. All of them can be assessed and the data can raise public awareness of any problems. Perhaps, as a knock-on effect, citizens may then protest for change. Personally, I'd love to see technology having this kind of effect on the world, and I think we can say that we're moving in the right direction.
Speaker 2	I couldn't agree more, David. People are really motivated by what improvements technology can offer. Going back to what you were saying about air quality, for example, knowing about this can help people make better decisions to improve their health.
Interviewer	Well, we have to leave it there. Thank you both for your interesting ideas.

Part 4

Audio track: C1_Listening_2_3_4.mp3

Part 4. You hear five short extracts in which people are talking about working in the music business. For questions 21 to 30, choose from the list A–H.

Extract 1	Both me and my wife work in the music business. In fact, I met her when she recorded in the studio I work in. We both love the profession, although we came to it by different routes. She's just a born talent, but I got my foot in the door after I got my qualification in sound engineering. I've been doing my job for almost ten years now, and I love it like I did on my first day. I suppose the hours aren't always great, but every day is different, and I get to work with some amazing people, even though a few may be a little demanding and precious!
Extract 2	My life might seem glamourous now, but it wasn't always like that. I only got noticed after I'd been singing around the office while doing some photocopies, and one of the producers working there heard me. I suppose it was destiny really! But it hasn't been all plain sailing: I've had four singles out now, and while they weren't all the successes that I'd hoped. It's hard to take the blows in this kind of business. It doesn't matter how talented you are sometimes – if your music doesn't get out there to the masses, it just won't do that well. I'm hoping I can tour soon and promote the next single more.
Extract 3	I really thought being a singer was a pipe dream, but I was nothing if not determined. My friends and I used to record in my mum's garage, and we'd pop our best efforts in the post, never imagining that anything would really come of it. We never thought that

Cambridge C1 Advanced Listening

someone would get in touch with us about it, but back in 1995 I was on my way to yet another audition when I got the call, and it's been a whirlwind ever since. I never thought we'd have so much success, but the band has been going from strength to strength. I've not had much time for a personal life, but that's the price to pay for following your dreams: being on the road and meeting all the fans.

Extract 4 When in was in my teens, I was mad about music and often took to the street with my guitar to play and make some money. One day a famous singer came past, spotted my talent and gave me the number of her manager – my life changed almost overnight. I've now worked with so many different artists and I tend to use a lot of classical samples for my work, but not as much as I'd like. My hands are often tied by what the businesspeople say will sell commercially. But I can't complain really: I've been all around the world and can live comfortably off something I really love.

Extract 5 I'd been trying to get into the music business for a long time, without any success, and I had almost given up on the idea. I started going for bit parts where there might be a chance to sing. Well, I went for a secondary role for some play and the producer heard me and introduced me to a contact at a record label! And that's how I ended up in a group, and our first album has just come out. There are absolutely no downsides to this job from what I can see… It doesn't even feel like a job! I know fame can be fleeting so I just hope we stay current, and the second album sells too.

Transcripts

Test 4

Part 1

Audio track: C1_Listening_2_4_1.mp3

Part 1. You will hear three different extracts. For questions 1 to 6, you must choose the best answer: A, B or C. There are two questions for each extract.

Extract 1	**You overhear a woman talking about her new house with a friend. Now look at questions 1 and 2.**
Speaker 1	I'm delighted with our new house you know. It's so spacious and has a lot of character – unlike that modern, soulless apartment we used to live in.
Speaker 2	I'm not surprised – you know, I've always wanted to live in a detached house like yours. There's something about not being connected to another building which really appeals to me.
Speaker 1	Yes, I see what you mean. Although there's quite a bit of work that needs to be done, as with all older houses I suppose.
Speaker 2	What are you going to start with?
Speaker 1	I think we're going to knock down a wall on the ground floor to expand the lounge as it doesn't get much light at the moment. We haven't really thought about decoration or colour schemes as we should really focus on the structural elements first.
Speaker 2	Don't you think you'll be removing some of the charm of the place by doing something like that? I mean, I know that open-plan is fashionable right now, but it might go out of date or look a bit odd.
Speaker 1	Yes, but I'm more interested in the building working for our needs rather than creating a museum piece. Some of the features of the house really need updating.
Extract 2	**You hear part of a conversation between a hotel employee and a guest. Now look at questions 3 and 4.**
Speaker 1	Hello, Sir. I'd just like to check whether you're enjoying your stay with us?
Speaker 2	Very much so. I mean it's not your average location, is it? I thought it was impressive when I first saw the pictures online, but I really wasn't anticipating this!
Speaker 1	Many of our guests have said that the photos don't really do it justice and you really have to experience it in person to fully appreciate the setting.
Speaker 2	Absolutely. It's so tranquil. It looks like something from a movie, and almost unreal in some respects.
Speaker 1	Nowhere else along this stretch of coastline can people witness the sunrise, as there aren't any other buildings for miles around.
Speaker 2	Oh really, why is that?
Speaker 1	We're in a national park you see, so the building of tourist accommodation is prohibited. This was an old farmhouse belonging to the previous landowner, and when

Cambridge C1 Advanced Listening

	the land was sold to the national park, special permission was granted to turn it into a hotel instead of demolishing it.
Speaker 2	Well, no wonder it attracts people from all over the place then. It's a truly unique setting and I shall recommend it without a doubt.
Speaker 1	Well, that would be most appreciated, sir. Thank you.

Extract 3	**You hear a radio interview with a scientist about sleep. Now look at questions 5 and 6.**
Speaker 1	I have Amy Cable, a scientist specialising in sleep, with me today to discuss why some people seem to need less sleep than others. Is this really true, or is there something else going on?
Speaker 2	Well, it may well be that they don't need quite as much sleep as the rest of us, but we should be cautious about these reports. I'd be sceptical if someone told me that they only needed four hours' sleep, for example.
Speaker 1	So, you're suggesting that these people are exaggerating what's going on because of some need to impress others?
Speaker 2	Perhaps. However, it's more likely that they've just miscalculated the amount of time they sleep. A possible explanation is that they're simply more efficient sleepers, and this could be attributed to fewer disruptions during the night. Many of us are woken up by noises, the need to go to the bathroom and so on.
Speaker 1	I sometimes find it difficult to get to sleep in the first place if I'm stressed or when I'm in a hotel with background noise which I'm not accustomed to.
Speaker 2	This could be an influencing factor, but science has a long way to go to get a definitive answer on this.

Part 2

Audio track: C1_Listening_2_4_2.mp3

Part 2. You hear a researcher called Chloe talking about first impressions. For questions 7 to 14, complete the sentences with a word or short phrase.

Today, I want to talk to you about my research into 'first impressions'. Now, it's very natural for people to feel nervous when meeting new people – after all, first impressions are important. We form judgements from the word go. But while making a good impression may feel like a trial for some, it doesn't need to be. In fact, my research indicates that we don't necessarily have to be dripping with natural charm. With just a little common sense, we can always make a reasonably good impact on new acquaintances.

Firstly, let's talk about eye contact. I can't stress the importance of this enough. We can easily see where someone is looking by noticing the movement of the eye. So, we can see if someone is giving us their attention or not, but people can also share their emotional states simply with their eyes. So, if you're full of confidence or friendliness when you look at someone, they'll feel it too!

Research has also found that eye contact can help keep our message in others' minds. On video calls, for instance, researchers have found that a direct gaze for thirty percent of the time is all it takes for participants to significantly increase their memory of the content of the call, although eye contact might not increase the *enjoyment* of the call – that very much depends on the content of the conversation.

Transcripts

When meeting someone new, our facial expressions are also important. Try to convey facially the effect you'd like to have on the other person. A smile is a great way to start, but make it natural. Research shows that a fake smile doesn't go unnoticed. Don't have a closed posture either. We often don't notice when we are doing things like crossing our arms, but it can seem very defensive.

The next thing I want to mention is the importance of preparation. If you have the chance beforehand, think about the situation you're going to be in and what you can talk about. Say, for example, you're going to a work conference and you'll need to meet new people and make a good impression. Make a list beforehand of interesting conversation starters you could ask. One natural topic could be their work life, but you can also ask questions about trivial topics like what they think of the catering. Now, some people say that you should avoid talking about personal lives, but it depends on where you draw the line. Apart from, perhaps, the topic of salary, I'd say anything goes!

This leads me naturally to my next point. Remember that communication is a two-way process, and to really make a good impression you've got to respond appropriately. Interruptions are a 'no-no'. Instead, listen to what the other person is saying and make sure your reaction indicates you've been listening. You could ask questions to show this. Also, provide non-verbal clues, like nodding to show your agreement or understanding of what is being said.

Lastly, be yourself. Remember why you want to make a good impression and don't contradict your true self. We're not all full of confidence after all. For example, if you're naturally shy you might not want to make lots of small talk, but you'll still have some abilities, like being able to look someone in the eye and/or simply smile. You can even make your weaknesses shown by saying that you're not very good in big groups. This is a way of deepening connections and can also encourage a genuine conversation.

Part 3

Audio track: C1_Listening_2_4_3.mp3

Part 3. You hear an interview in which two conservationists are talking about birds. For questions 15 to 20, choose the best answer: A, B, C or D.

Interviewer	Welcome to Animal Matters where today we're discussing how climate change is affecting bird numbers and what we should be doing about it. With me are conservationists Philippa Knight and Matteo Erikson. Are you both optimistic about the future of our feathery friends?
Speaker 1	Well, it depends on the location and the species. Although we hear a lot about the number of species that are at risk of extinction or endangered, in some parts of the world things are definitely moving in the right direction.
Speaker 2	Indeed. It's important to look on the bright side even though the news headlines are pretty negative about the number of birds that have been lost in recent decades.
Speaker 1	You know, people all over the world are doing an outstanding job of increasing populations. One example is the Californian condor. It's a majestic bird, larger than an eagle, and until conservationists stepped in it was heading for extinction. Now there are over 300 in the wild and many more in captive breeding programmes in zoos.
Interviewer	Oh, wow that is impressive. Do you have any examples you'd like to discuss, Matteo?
Speaker 2	Well, I'd like to see the limited time and money we have diverted to less impressive birds. Like the fruit dove, for example, which plays a vital role in ecosystems. This tiny bird disperses the seeds of fruit trees in the rainforests of Southeast Asia, and therefore has an impact on the survival of other creatures too.
Speaker 1	I agree to some extent, but by focusing on the more impressive species, like condors and eagles, we can raise the profile of bird protection in general. If we can attract people's attention, and they can see how a concerted effort makes a difference to a

Cambridge C1 Advanced Listening

	seriously endangered species, then maybe they'll get on board with programmes in their neighbourhoods, irrespective of the species.
Interviewer	And how do people get involved with this kind of thing, Matteo?
Speaker 2	Start by looking online for local conservation organisations to join. In my area, for example, there is a bird-watch group that monitors bird boxes in the park. We record the numbers in spring and send them to the national bird-tracking group. Although it sounds like this isn't much, huge amounts of data are being amassed, which is extremely valuable to scientists mapping bird-population changes.
Interviewer	How interesting. Are there any other benefits of these local projects, Phillippa?
Speaker 1	Actually, this kind of proactivity can encourage our local politicians to create better policies or even nationwide programmes. I know that in Canada, for example, there's a large programme where cities can get a certificate to say they're 'bird friendly'. Residents can learn about how certain types of buildings and pets are a threat and what they can do to address this.
Interviewer	Like nets, you mean?
Speaker 2	No, these are not recommended because birds can easily become trapped in them – not to mention the fact that they are expensive and difficult to maintain. An alternative is to simply install glass with a pattern or apply a covering to the outside of the window. These come in different sizes for large public and office buildings as well as for your home.
Interviewer	And how can people attract more birds into their gardens?
Speaker 1	Encouraging more birds is surprisingly straightforward and need not cost the earth either. Putting up bird boxes for shelter and avoiding the use of pesticides are easy actions you can take. And with just a little more research and investment of time you could grow insect-friendly plants.
Interviewer	Well, thank you both. This has been fascinating.

Part 4

Audio track: C1_Listening_2_4_4.mp3

Part 4. You hear five short extracts in which people are talking about using social media at work. For questions 21 to 30, choose from the list A–H.

Extract 1	Working for myself, I use social media quite a lot. It's an essential way of keeping in touch with the industry I work in and finding out what's hot and what's not, but that's not my main focus for it. I use it mainly as a showcase for my own work, so that as many people as possible know who I am. I always try to use the personal touch on social media, because I want to make people feel engaged. So I always make sure to post something in response to a positive comment. And I also try to deal with any negativity – and there's always that ONE person – in a way that isn't aggressive. I can't afford to come across badly.
Extract 2	Social media is a great way to highlight our products, but it's also one of the first places customers come to if something doesn't reach their expectations. Essentially, making these people satisfied with the final outcome is what I do ninety percent of the time. Of course, it's not just up to me, thankfully. There are official steps we need to follow as an organisation, and these were provided by people who really know how to deal with large customer numbers. Getting in this kind of outside knowledge is essential when working in social media for your organisation. They've checked every box in terms of research, so you don't need to!

Extract 3 The multinational I work for is a household name in at least 50 countries across the world, and I'm part of a team that works in the social media department. It's our job to ensure that essentially all the quality and values we're known for are transmitted in our social media presence. This keeps our customer base secure in the knowledge that we'll always be there. It's not tricky to get the tone right for us – we have a standard way of writing things – but we do make sure we go through everything carefully. I for one can't stand a typo! It's always a good idea to keep an eye out for that kind of thing, but it's a great way to earn a living.

Extract 4 Companies come to me to find out what certain groups of people think about their products – people that represent their potential customers – and social media has made this far easier. I get lots more responses online, but I've also got to be careful to not flood certain groups with too many requests. I choose different customer bases for different things, which helps, but one thing that most people dislike is feeling overwhelmed by one company. I always remember that when posting!

Extract 5 I've been quite big on social media for some time. I've got a huge following of people, and every time I post another money-saving tip I get thousands of likes. I've managed to generate a good income from this too, and people sign up to my newsletter. First and foremost, though, I think I provide a good service. It's not easy to get started and gain a profile on social media. You've got to think outside the box to stand out as there are thousands of people flooding the internet with the very same ideas as you. Post regularly, and post great, engaging content.

Cambridge C1 Advanced Listening

Test 5

Part 1

Audio track: C1_Listening_2_5_1.mp3

Part 1. You will hear three different extracts. For questions 1 to 6, you must choose the best answer: A, B or C. There are two questions for each extract.

Extract 1	**You hear two writers discussing inspiration. Now look at questions 1 and 2.**
Speaker 1	Whenever I do writers' workshops, I get asked about how I find inspiration, but it's quite hard to pin that down. So I just do some exercises to help the audience explore where inspiration could come from.
Speaker 2	Hmm, I think many people expect to have 'lightbulb moments', when actually I find that most sources of inspiration are drawn from unusual events or chance conversations.
Speaker 1	For me, it's often reading – especially lifestyle magazines or things I come across online by accident.
Speaker 2	To my mind, the issue is that inexperienced writers are looking for some kind of formula to follow, when writing is quite a messy business with bits that flow and times of frustration.
Speaker 1	And inspiration doesn't always lead to a good story or an interesting article because it can be too specific and therefore lack universal appeal.
Speaker 2	That's a good point. I'd like to feature that in my next workshop if that is okay with you.
Extract 2	**You hear a man talking about applying for a promotion with a colleague. Now look at questions 3 and 4.**
Speaker 1	Have you heard about the vacancy for the supervisor role in the finance department? I've been pondering whether to apply or not because ever since I completed my accounting diploma, I've been feeling like I'm not really being stretched any more.
Speaker 2	Yeah, you could, but if I were you I'd definitely consider looking elsewhere as well. There are some good opportunities in the labour market at the moment, and lots of organisations are recruiting. With your skills, I'm sure you could do better than sticking around here.
Speaker 1	But the supervisor role would give me a chance to get some experience on the next rung of the career ladder without having to go through all the upheaval of changing company. Not to mention the fact that the perks are attractive – performance bonuses, gym membership and some other stuff too.
Speaker 2	Hmm, that's true I suppose, but do you think it would be challenging enough in the long run? With everything here being so familiar, you might find yourself frustrated all over again and wishing you'd moved on earlier.
Speaker 1	Well, that's assuming I get the job! There are quite a few members of the department who probably think they'd be more suitable than me!
Extract 3	**You hear a conversation between two friends about social media. Now look at questions 5 and 6.**

Speaker 1	I came across a video online the other day talking about how our generation is wasting time on social media and how we'll regret it when we're older. I mean, there were some good points but a lot of them seemed a bit dramatic.
Speaker 2	People are always saying things like that, and I take issue with some of the claims. I mean, how much time exactly do they mean, and is it wasted time if I'm discovering interesting things or engaging with others?
Speaker 1	Well, I suppose it's different for everyone. I've decided to get rid of lots of distracting stuff on my phone, and I've uninstalled some of my social apps as an experiment to see whether I can manage without them.
Speaker 2	In my opinion, social media isn't always at fault, it's perfectly fine and fulfils a need for communication and entertainment and is usually quite harmless. Obviously, for some, it takes up more time than it should, but they're in the minority.
Speaker 1	I think I'm just scrolling through things when I can't motivate myself to study or do something more constructive.
Speaker 2	Well, I'll be interested to see how you get on and what you end up doing with all this extra time you're going to have.

Part 2

Audio track: C1_Listening_2_5_2.mp3

Part 2. You hear a woman called Monica talking about her job in the film industry. For questions 7 to 14, complete the sentences with a word or short phrase.

Today, I'm going to tell you about working behind the screen in the film industry – in particular, my job: script supervision.

My role is very complicated as I'm the person who ensures all the details of the film are correct. While the director runs the overall production, he or she also needs a surrounding team. These roles can range from a consultant on art to a personal assistant, or, like me, simply a backup to ensure everything is as it should be. I need to make sure that what the director has in mind is what we're actually shooting.

The job involves a lot of watching, listening and taking notes. So, for example, I'll listen to directions given during rehearsals and help the director remember these when it comes to filming. I need to watch for everything, so if there are small changes – for example, an actor who says something differently – it's up to me to notice that and record it.

What makes this task even more challenging is how we film. It would be ideal to shoot scenes in the order of the story. Unfortunately, it's often impractical as we've got to cater for location costs and cast availability. So, everything is often shot out of sequence. I've got to make sure everything makes sense, nothing gets missed, and that it can all be sewn together in the final edit. It's a lot!

Because of this, I need to write down everything that happens on set – and I mean *everything* – and send it to the post-production team. Obviously, it's important to follow the script, but it's far more essential that the final edit makes sense – whether it's true to the original or not – as the script can evolve during production. My notes often end up being hundreds of pages long!

I usually have to start preparing long before filming begins. I need to have time to read the script carefully, breaking it down scene by scene. Also, the director and director of photography will have a

Cambridge C1 Advanced Listening

vision for the film, which I really need to have clear in my head too. Once I've got this, I can analyse the script in terms of cast, actions, wardrobe and props.

We might have a scene that is based on the same day in a film, but in production we're filming it ten days apart. All you need is for just one thing to be out of place and people will notice it. In the film 'Forrest Gump', as Forrest is finding out about his son, we can see an ironing board in the background – the iron moves positions as the scene switches from the son watching TV and back to the parents. I need to prevent errors like that.

So, what do you need to do become a script supervisor? Well, you don't always need to have been a media student, although a relevant media qualification always helps. In general, it's best to try and get experience working on a film, especially in film production. A junior-level role like a production assistant is a great place to begin your career, as you can build contacts and work your way up from there. You can then go on to be an assistant director among many other roles. Script supervision isn't for everyone.

Lastly, I want to let you know how great it is working in the industry. There are so many interesting people working on a set, so it's generally a pretty exciting place to work. It's also demanding, however, with long hours and tight deadlines, and job security isn't always guaranteed as there's plenty of competition. But don't let the downsides put you off. I wouldn't change a thing about my job really!

Part 3

Audio track: C1_Listening_2_5_3.mp3

Part 3. You hear part of a radio discussion in which two food writers are talking about their interest in global tea culture. For questions 15 to 20, choose the best answer: A, B, C or D.

Speaker 1	Trends in food and drink come and go all the time, yet one of the world's most consistently loved drinks is tea. I know that a lot of food historians are intrigued by some of the more controversial aspects of its history. For me, it's the historical significance – you know, the traditions which have grown up around it over the years. But I'm keen to know what got you interested in the subject, Oliver?
Speaker 2	Well, Leah, while on holiday in China a few years ago I stumbled upon the National Tea Museum quite by chance. And the section on medicinal uses really grabbed my attention. At that time, I'd just started out as a food journalist, and I really thought I would end up focusing on the rise of vegetarianism as that was in the headlines a lot. So that visit was a complete turning point.
Speaker 1	And have you continued to focus on that particular aspect, or have you moved on?
Speaker 2	Once I wrote a historical book about tea superstitions and beliefs that developed in 18th-century Britain. But apart from that, my writing tends to be from a well-being perspective. Recently, I've done a few magazine pieces on the trend of drinking tea for digestive and mental health. I've found researching this really interesting because it feels like a reflection of its original roots in ancient Asian cultures when tea was prized for its health-giving properties.
Speaker 1	Precisely! It was a high-status drink when first introduced into European societies in the 19th Century – and then went on to become a common and inexpensive beverage for the masses in 20th-century Britain. Now, it's like we've come full circle and people have realised what tea can do for us again.
Speaker 2	Incidentally, I also write articles examining other cultural practices like gift-giving and hospitality. Many cultures use tea in a kind of ceremonial or ritual sense – sometimes more formally like the famed tea ceremony in Japan, but also in a more informal setting like in Morocco or Turkey as a way to strengthen and maintain personal relationships. My writing has taken me to all sorts of places investigating how these

Transcripts

practices have remained or if they are disappearing.

Speaker 1 I do think a lot is written about tea traditions which is misleading. Over the last couple of decades or so generational differences have appeared in many places. Especially as vast swathes of young people have become coffee fans all over the globe. I sometimes suspect that these days some of those so-called 'long-standing traditions' are being kept alive just for the tourists.

Speaker 2 Right, well I mean we can see consumer trends changing in all sorts of ways. Look at the situation with loose-leaf tea, for example. It's on the rise as tea bags become less popular with the more environmentally conscious. And, of course, fair-trade tea is widely available in supermarkets as well as in speciality tea stores now.

Speaker 1 I do wonder whether that's the whole story, though. I suspect that nowadays companies are more than happy to use environmental factors to sell a new brand of tea, however flimsy they may be. But finally, Oliver, what do you think we'll be writing about in the future when it comes to tea?

Speaker 2 I feel like we've probably reached somewhat of a cultural dead end, but there's real excitement about some of the science going on. Until recently, not much was known about the chemical compounds in tea, for instance. Many recent studies have shown how they seem to ward off disease or at least reduce it.

Speaker 1 Okay, so we'll keep our eyes peeled for some mysteries to be uncovered soon.

Part 4

Audio track: C1_Listening_2_5_4.mp3

Part 4. You hear five short extracts in which people are talking about their gap year. For questions 21 to 30, choose from the list A–H.

Extract 1 When I was thinking about going on a gap year, I was desperate to see the world, but the practicalities of it meant I couldn't afford to just take off and have fun with my friends. I spoke a bit of Italian and found a temporary position in Milan. I spent a lot of my day making beds and washing sheets, but I had a fantastic time. If I could do it again, I'd try not to be quite so concerned about money and do something that meant I could sit back and enjoy the experience more before the hard study at university started.

Extract 2 I decided to take a gap year so I could find out what life is like in a completely different place. I spent the year in Ankara where I didn't speak a word of English for the entire time I was there, and it was an incredible way to pick up Turkish. I lived with a family, spending time with the children and seeing the city. I wouldn't change a thing about it. I think considering your interests and doing something related to them is far better than just thinking of a gap year as an extended holiday travelling around with a bunch of friends. What are you going to learn from that, after all?

Extract 3 I've always wanted to go into some kind of caring profession, whether it be for animals or children, and I knew I wanted to do something related to that. I ended up in Malaysia – a beautiful country – working with kids in a rural school where normally they wouldn't have to speak English. It didn't pay much, but it was enough to see the country and more. If I had to give someone advice for their gap year, I would say don't stay in your comfort zone. It's a perfect time to try new things and find out who you are and what you might like to do in the future.

Cambridge C1 Advanced Listening

Extract 4 I had a fantastic gap year. I ended up going to about twelve different countries and managed to fund it by working remotely for my dad's charity at the same time. It was just part-time work, but it certainly enabled me to fund my travels. I made some great friends, and I also got to go outward bound and see some of the countryside. The one thing that was essential to me was making sure I could budget for every step and every adventure that I had. If you're smart, you'll be amazed by how much you can do with so little!

Extract 5 I really wanted to do something out of the ordinary on my gap year, so instead of staying in hotels or hostels I decided to go one step further and headed out to the Brazilian rainforest. I used a compass, made fires to cook on – things I'd never even dreamed of doing back home. The land and the array of animals there are pretty amazing, and although I wouldn't recommend it to just anyone, it was perfect for me. If you want to do something adventurous like this, make sure you consider the situations you might find yourself in – thankfully, the guides are pretty experienced, but the more you know beforehand the better.

Transcripts

Test 6

Part 1

Audio track: C1_Listening_2_6_1.mp3

Part 1. You will hear three different extracts. For questions 1 to 6, you must choose the best answer: A, B or C. There are two questions for each extract.

Extract 1 **You hear a discussion between a tour guide and a tourist. Now look at questions 1 and 2.**

Speaker 1 I'd recommend the hike up to the waterfall, as long as you've got appropriate clothing and footwear. We get sudden rains at this time of year so the ground can get a little slippery.

Speaker 2 I'm guessing you wouldn't advise doing this with a couple of teenagers who can be accident-prone, then?

Speaker 1 If it was during the dry season, I'd say it would be fine, but in July it might be a bit treacherous, and I wouldn't take the risk if I were you. The path up to the volcano is more accessible, and the volcano isn't active so there's no danger there.

Speaker 2 Hmm, the kids might quite like that, actually. I don't think they've ever seen volcanic rock before. I could probably persuade them that it would be an adventure and not like a school field trip! They've got a compass and some plant- and insect-identification apps to keep them occupied as they walk.

Speaker 1 Great. At the summit, there's a visitor centre, although you need to call in advance if you want the guided tour. If the truth be told, it's all perfectly self-explanatory unless you're *really* into geology.

Extract 2 **You hear a woman telling a friend about finding a childhood toy. Now look at questions 3 and 4.**

Speaker 1 Since retiring, my parents have decided to sell up so my sister and I went round to lend a hand with packing and sorting through various unwanted possessions.

Speaker 2 I bet they were grateful. It must be daunting after having lived somewhere for several decades and accumulating so much.

Speaker 1 Absolutely. Anyway, while we were clearing out the attic, we discovered a train set still in remarkable condition considering that we weren't always that gentle when playing with it.

Speaker 2 Oh, that must have been a wonderful surprise! These days, there's a thriving collectors' market for childhood toys so it might be worth your while having it valued.

Speaker 1 Well, I'm not sure it could be considered an antique because it's not as old as it looks. It was modelled on an old-fashioned version that was famous at the turn of the 20th Century. I mean, it's a good copy but I don't think it'd fool a professional dealer.

Speaker 2 You could see if any of the neighbourhood children are interested so at least you'll know it's gone to a good home.

Speaker 1 Actually, I didn't realise that it would bring back so many precious memories, so rather than just giving it away I'd prefer to see if our kids are interested in it first.

Cambridge C1 Advanced Listening

Extract 3 — **You hear part of an interview with a TV presenter about her new show. Now look at questions 5 and 6.**

Speaker 1 — I'm joined on the Breakfast Show this morning by Christina Harrison, TV presenter and producer, and she's going to tell us about her new show, which is a documentary series about modern society.

Speaker 2 — Hi Graham, and thanks for having me on today. I'm really excited about this new programme, and I think it'll appeal to a wide audience because it investigates things like the importance of community or how technology is shaping the world.

Speaker 1 — But this is very much new territory for you, isn't it? How did you make the move from fronting a local news programme to this?

Speaker 2 — Yes, I admit that this new role is a far cry from that, but I suppose I'd been wanting to broaden my horizons for a while. I thought I'd take the initiative and audition for some different roles and see what happened.

Speaker 1 — Well, judging by the reviews of the first two programmes in the series, that has paid off. People seem to like your relaxed style of interviewing experts.

Speaker 2 — I think that being new to all this actually gives me an advantage because viewers don't have any expectations of me, and, also, I think my style helps put the guests at ease.

Part 2

Audio track: C1_Listening_2_6_2.mp3

Part 2. You hear a researcher called Jane talking about exploring the deep sea. For questions 7 to 14, complete the sentences with a word or short phrase.

So, today I want to speak to you about my life researching the deep sea. Ever since I was a little kid, I've always been fascinated by the sea, and had watched lots of programmes about it. But it wasn't until we went on holiday, and I managed to explore a coral reef myself, that I decided to dedicate my life to it.

Years ago, it wasn't at all easy to actually get down to the very deep sea, but that all changed with the development of a deep-sea submersible named ALVIN. I've been working with *him* since the early 70s. It might sound strange that I refer to ALVIN as a he, but actually giving the submersible a name has humanised it to many of us researchers. He's been updated so many times that he doesn't have any of his original parts, although little has changed about his objectives – more than 3,000 people have been down into the depths in ALVIN, and he's an invaluable research tool.

Although you might not know it, you've probably seen ALVIN's work. He was the submersible sent down to get the extraordinary footage of the *Titanic* in 1986 – the very first footage since the ship sunk in 1912. ALVIN at first focussed on the bow section, and then found the rear section around 60 metres away. The submersible remained on the deck of the ship, while a remotely operated machine focused on getting footage of both the inside and outside of the wreck.

While this is the highest-profile set of dives, ALVIN has done so much more, and is an invaluable tool for research with his ability to access around 99% of the ocean floor. Diving in ALVIN is a transformative experience. The pilots turn the lights off on the descent, in order to conserve energy, then, when you're near the bottom, everything is lit up so you can do the research. It's not cheap or easy to get ALVIN to the ocean floor – you usually need to do tasks for not only your research but also others.

Transcripts

There are only three people who can travel on ALVIN: the pilot and two scientists – the port observer, who is in charge of the research elements, and the starboard observer, who assists and takes notes. I've done both scientific roles in my time, and in my opinion they are equally important and exciting roles.

Our jobs, and what we use to collect samples, are quite varied. The type of area we need to sample, and our research aims, define what collection methods we need to use. For example, in my last trip we sampled life on a coral site. This involved using a net to collect a sample of a specific area, but we don't use nets in cold water sites. We were down there for seven hours, and the time flew. Usually, we need to get everything done by the ascent time, but most of the work actually happens when we're back on the main ship, as then we have to process all of the samples in the labs.

On a more practical note, there's not much space in ALVIN – not even space for a toilet – and taking care of the environment is very important. As such, when we're down there, we can bring a sandwich for lunch, but we can't take our phones, or in fact citrus fruits. If you peel an orange, the oils that come off it might ignite in the presence of pure oxygen, and no one wants that in an enclosed space under the sea!

Part 3

Audio track: C1_Listening_2_6_3.mp3

Part 3. You hear part of a radio discussion about cycling schemes with two experts in cycling and safety. For questions 15 to 20, choose the best answer: A, B, C or D.

Interviewer	Today, we're talking about the impact of cycle schemes in cities. I'm joined by Julian Reeves from the National Cycle Network and Gina Maddison from the Road Safety Association. I'd like to start with safety, actually, so, Gina, can you talk us through how these schemes have affected road safety?
Speaker 1	Sure. And thanks for having me. I think the effects have been overwhelmingly positive. Interestingly, a lot of this has to do with what is called 'a positive feedback loop' rather than statistics. Remember that accident rates often go up just because more people fall off bikes, but these are usually minor injuries. Anyway, this feedback loop occurs when people perceive streets with fewer cars as being safer, so they cycle more, even on streets which are not necessarily safer. Others then think that more cyclists mean safer streets and cyclist numbers increase even more.
Interviewer	Ah, I see. And you've done some research on a different aspect relating to how road users think, haven't you, Julian?
Speaker 2	Oh, you're referring to the delivery driver example. You know, I think this is really intriguing. Delivery drivers are often some of the fiercest campaigners against cycle schemes at first because there's this assumption that the roads will be full of slow-moving bicycles. However, when they observed a reduction in travel times that meant they could squeeze in more deliveries, they came around to the idea pretty quickly.
Interviewer	How do you both feel about the speed of implementation? I mean, many citizens around the world complain that not enough is being done and it's too slow.
Speaker 2	I think it's essential to mention that they shouldn't be implemented without a thorough analysis of their suitability. For a start, it's important to think about the terrain – and the flatter the better. I know some cities have had success with e-bikes, but this does require more investment and so is not available to everyone.
Speaker 1	And that's why consultation is so important. You have to get experts in traffic and safety in to look at what can and can't be achieved. You can't just introduce a cycle scheme and expect accident numbers to disappear if you haven't also redesigned some of the city.
Interviewer	And how does this kind of thing actually get put into practice?

Cambridge C1 Advanced Listening

Speaker 1 You have to start with some basic infrastructure, like special cycle paths, and signs need to change to make drivers aware of cyclists. Then, you have to work on lighting at night and payment points, as well as logistics. What a lot of people don't realise about cycle schemes is that trucks have to move the bicycles around at night, so they are distributed across the city again ready for the next day.

Interviewer Ah, yes. I see what you mean. Does the weather also have an impact on this?

Speaker 2 That's a good point, and yes it does. Good cycle-scheme management means liaising with other government departments. Roads need to be cleared of leaves and ice in colder seasons to maintain cycle-lane safety in the same way as roads are. It's not just a case of setting everything up and expecting it to be fine.

Interviewer And are there any other challenges that organisations such as yours face when trying to get people on board with cycle schemes?

Speaker 2 Certain groups of people can be difficult to convince, and this is often because they can't see how the scheme will work in their neighbourhood. We always focus on how a scheme will improve the lives of local residents.

Speaker 1 I'd say that it's about doing things properly so that they're integrated into the town or city and work for everyone. There is no one-size-fits-all solution.

Part 4

Audio track: C1_Listening_2_6_4.mp3

Part 4. You hear five short extracts in which people are talking about learning to cook. For questions 21 to 30, choose from the list A–H.

Extract 1 I really hadn't shown much interest in food until I was diagnosed with a food allergy and I realised I'd have to cook for myself and be more careful. There were precious few books on cooking the way I needed to cook, but fortunately I managed to find plenty of blogs about it and basically picked it up from there. It's not until you make your own food that you realise all the stuff that's packed into most processed foods. Half of it is junk! At least when you're doing the cooking you can make sure you're using decent ingredients, even if it can often take more time and money to do it that way.

Extract 2 I'd always enjoyed going to other people's houses when I was young, because they cooked proper food. My parents were hopeless and almost everything we ate was out of a packet! So, when I got to university I wasn't just learning in my classes. I also decided to buy fresh ingredients and try to make dishes up from scratch. Although there were a few horrors, I think I had a natural ability, and I've learnt a lot more from all kinds of places. It's now become a hobby, and I find it a terrific way to unwind, when I have the time.

Extract 3 Cooking is quite a mystery when you don't know how to do it, and it's something that might seem overwhelming to learn at first, but I had no choice but to learn at speed when I got a job serving school dinners – and I had no idea: I spent the evenings before I started in front of the Cookery Channel hoping the techniques would stick so I could go in there on my first day with some knowledge. Of course, in those kinds of kitchens you can't be very inventive – it's all organisation and process – but it's certainly taken away my self-doubt in the kitchen. Now, all my family can't wait to sit down to dinner!

Extract 4 I wouldn't say I particularly enjoy cooking. Certainly not when I was a child when I'd be dragged into the kitchen to make cookies or something similar. But I've got to say those skills have come in handy later in life. I suppose it's good to know I can draw on my own abilities and not have to simply eat what someone else cooks for me. It's a long way from fun for me, but it's useful nevertheless. I'd rather order a takeaway most of the time, though, if I'm honest. I much prefer someone else to do the cooking, even if it's more expensive that way!

Extract 5   Around five years ago, my maximum level of cooking was boiling an egg! When I picked up recipe books I always seemed to get overwhelmed with the instructions, and it never turned out like the pictures. So, I decided I'd need some face-to-face help, which I found in the local college. After going twice a week for ten weeks, I'm now a pretty decent cook. And, even better, I've cut my supermarket bill in half just by buying raw ingredients instead of packet after packet of ready meals.